TRAIN THE BRAVE

BE YOUR BEST

TRAIN THE BRAVE

Tame Your Fear, Take the Chance, Dare To Live Big

MARGIE WARRELL

WILEY

First published as *Brave* in 2015 by John Wiley & Sons Australia, Ltd
42 McDougall St, Milton Qld 4064
Office also in Melbourne
This edition first published in 2019 by John Wiley & Sons Australia, Ltd

Typeset in 12.5/14.5pt Arno Pro

NATIONAL LIBRARY OF AUSTRALIA

A catalogue record for this book is available from the National Library of Australia

Printed in Singapore by C.O.S. Printers Pte Ltd

Author photo: Alise Black

V224540_022619

ISBN 978-0-730-36943-1

Margie sets herself apart with a powerful and inspiring message, paired with her energetic, down-to-earth and disarming delivery. Margie's insights helped me bolster my personal vision for a candid, collaborative and forward-leaning workplace. She provided practical advice on how to challenge ourselves and others to be more courageous, take more risks and find more success.

Kathy Calvin, President and CEO,
United Nations Foundation

Nothing worthwhile is achieved living timidly and avoiding all risk. *Train the Brave* will help you build the confidence to dare more boldly and live more bravely.

Carolyn Cresswell, Company Founder and
Managing Director, Carman's Kitchen

Fear and doubt are the two greatest enemies to success in business and life. Written for busy people on the go, this practical and encouraging book will guide you to achieve your greatest goals in work and life.

Kate Carnell AO, CEO Australian Chamber
of Commerce and Industry

Train the Brave will help you grow your 'courage muscles' to achieve your biggest dreams and wildest ambitions. Read it often. Practise it daily.

Emma Isaacs, CEO, Business Chicks

If you have ever doubted your ability to achieve these wildly big goals, you don't need to any longer! *Train the Brave* needs to become your most valuable book as it will give you useful insight, tips and tricks to ensure you live your life fully!

Paul McKeown, Head of Retail,
The Body Shop

Many people doubt themselves too much, and back themselves too little (particularly us women!). If you want to live more bravely, more boldly, and more fully, this book was written for you! It's a game changer.

Deborah Hutton, media personality

A unique blend of the practical and inspirational, *Train the Brave* will help you overcome the fears and doubts that are holding you back in your career, business, relationships and life.

Joe Powell, Managing Director,
SEEK Employment & Learning

Courage is the basis for all success. Without bravery and courage you can go through life making excuses about why you can't or shouldn't do things. Our first instinct is often to say no as it's easier and feels safer. But true courage comes from saying YES — to yourself, your ambitions and your happiness. Read this book and you'll be on your way to a bigger, braver and more fulfilling life. Enjoy.

Janine Allis, Founder of Boost Juice and
Executive Director, Retail Zoo

Courage is more needed than ever in today's 'play it safe' world, where taking the soft option can be all too easy. This book will help you to build the courage needed to do the right thing rather than the easy thing — to go out on a limb, have tough conversations, challenge the norm and risk failing. It should be read widely.

Michael O'Keefe, CEO, Aesop

Train the Brave is better than a book — it's a manual for life full of wise, useful and actionable advice that only an author who has earned her stripes — through triumph and tragedy — could write. Be braver. This book will show you how.

Bill Treasurer, author of *Right Risk* and
CEO, Giant Leap Consulting

Train the Brave is the handbook you need to start living your life more purposefully, passionately and courageously. No more holding yourself back or dimming yourself down! You deserve a life you love and this book will help you live it!

Michelle McQuaid, best-selling author of
Your Strengths Blueprint

Contents

About the author

Find Your Courage, Stop Playing Safe, Make Your Mark.

The titles of Margie's three other bestselling books reflect her passion for helping people make braver decisions and lead bigger lives.

Margie's had to find her courage many times since growing up, one of seven children, on a small farm in rural Australia. Personal struggles, family tragedies, an armed robbery, four children in five years: all have taught her valuable lessons on embracing change, building resilience and conquering fear.

Today Margie draws on her background in business, coaching and psychology to help people thrive in work, leadership and life. Her clients include NASA, Berkshire Hathaway, Facebook, Johnson & Johnson, Mars, Microsoft, Oracle, and the United Nations Foundation.

Host of the Live Brave Podcast, Margie's insights have also been shaped by interviews with leaders and luminaries such as Sir Richard Branson, Steve Forbes, Bill Marriott and Marianne Williamson.

An acclaimed international speaker, Margie is also a member of the Advisory Board of Forbes School of Business & Technology, a Women's Economic Forum honoree and a sought-after commentator with leading media such as *The Wall Street Journal*, Bloomberg, Fox News, the *Today* show and *Inc. Magazine*.

Margie does her best to talk her talk when it comes to living bravely. An adventurer by heart, she has crossed the Sahara desert, stayed in Palestinian refugee camps, cycled the streets of Beijing, hiked the Inca trail, spent three years living in Papua New Guinea and most recently climbed Mt Kilimanjaro with her husband and four equally intrepid children.

For more information and inspiration, visit margiewarrell.com.

Acknowledgements

Every book involves an act of courage in some measure. This book is no exception and so I want to acknowledge the many people who've supported me in the journey to bring *Train the Brave* into your hands.

To Lucy Raymond, my editor at Wiley. When I first mentioned the idea of writing this book, with its short focused chapters, and which didn't fall squarely with Wiley's core 'business book' genre, I held little confidence it would be of interest to them. More personal than my previous book *Stop Playing Safe*, this book has therefore been not just an act of bravery for me, but for Wiley which has backed it. So Lucy, a heartfelt thank you for your faith in me and in this book! Thank you also to the whole team at Wiley and my delightful (and patient!) editor Sandra Balonyi. Once again, you have enabled me to share my passion and insights more broadly through the words in this book.

I can't let it go without mentioning that during with the writing of this updated acknowledgements I am preparing to celebrate 21 years of marriage with my husband Andrew (yes, a child bride!). While the longevitiy of a marriage doesn't necessarily reflect the love within it, I'm very fortunate to have married someone who has always been my most ardent champion. So to Andrew, thank you. Our lives are often extremely busy as we now straddle three hemispheres pursuing our dreams and nurturing our children to pursue their own, yet you always make time for me — to bounce ideas off, encourage me, counter my doubts and point out where I'm selling myself short. You've helped me to 'train my brave' countless times and I cannot imagine how I'd ever become the woman I am had I not had you by my side.

Acknowledgement also to our four exceedingly loveable and big-spirited children: Lachlan, Maddy, Ben and Matthew. Twelve years ago, when I began writing my first book, *Find Your Courage*, you were aged seven and under, and still watching The Wiggles. During the writing of this book one of you left home and one of you jumped out of a plane with a parachute (landing safely!). While I sometimes feel sad that this family-rich season of my life is passing so quickly, I could not be more proud of the brave-hearted, passionate, adventurous and good-humoured young adults who call me 'Mum'. Keep shining brightly as you each pursue the boldest vision for your lives.

A big shout out also to my 'support crew' around the globe for your invaluable behind-the-scenes support. While I have now moved away, thank you also to George, Jason, Sam, Peter and all the crew at the White Rabbit cafe in Brighton for letting me set up permanent residence at the back corner table. You make the best lattes in Melbourne!

Of course, I'm also immensely grateful to my family, friends and 'followers' — online and offline — whose support is always, always, appreciated. We can go so much further together than we ever can alone, so thank you for inspiring me to think bigger and live braver. Yes, I know that's grammatically incorrect but, as I write in this book, rules can be soooo over-rated!

And last, but not least, thank you to my beautiful dad and mum, Ray and Maureen Kleinitz. You gave me deep roots, strong wings and profound faith in a higher Power far greater than my own. Knowing that you would have been proud of me no matter what I did has freed me to follow my heart in all matters, to live purposefully and to pursue work I love. What a different world we would live in if every child could grow up feeling so unconditionally loved. It's my deepest hope that this book will help to bring greater love into more hearts, peace into more homes, and, in some small way, joy into more lives. If it does, then know you played your part.

Margie

Introduction

How many times have you kept your mouth shut when there was something you really wanted to say? How often have you held back from doing something for fear of failing or appearing foolish? When did you 'go along to get along', only to regret it later? Do you sometimes tell yourself that you're not smart enough, strong enough or brave enough to make that change or take that chance?

If you've ever thought to yourself, 'If I just had the guts', you're not alone.

None of us is immune to fear — of failing, criticism, rejection or being 'found out' as unworthy in some way. Yet, left unchecked, our fears can confine our lives in countless ways. Which is why living fully is synonymous with living bravely: being willing to back yourself and take a risk, speak your truth and exit your comfort zone to go after what you truly want, change what you don't and honour yourself fully.

PLAYING SAFE AND AVOIDING RISK DOESN'T MAKE US MORE SECURE, IT MAKES US LESS SO.

The truth is that living bravely is not easy. If it were, we all would be! There's no magic formula or pain-free, 10-step plan to permanently liberate yourself from fear. The only way to be brave is to act bravely — day in, day out — when times are easy and life feels good *and* when times are tough and it doesn't. It's why I've written this book: to help you strengthen your muscles for living bravely. Not just because of what you can accomplish when you do, but because of who you will become in the process. Stronger. Wiser. Happier. More purposeful. More resilient. And more whole. As E. E. Cummings once wrote, 'It takes courage to grow up and become who you really are'.

I discovered the power of 'training the brave' while learning how to ride horses growing up on a small dairy farm in rural Australia. I was six the first time I got on a horse at our local show. It was very exciting but ... oh ... the ground seemed so far down. With each lap of the pony ring, my fear began to abate, so much so that by the time I was being plucked off the saddle I'd decided that riding horses wasn't so scary after all (at least not small ones).

Being relatively isolated from the activities available to city kids, I decided to try my luck in soliciting my parents to buy me a pony for my tenth birthday. I had no great expectation I'd get one. A drought had meant that money was tight, but my dad managed to get enough dollars together to buy me an old, beginner-friendly gelding named Roby. He arrived on the back of Dad's old cattle trailer the day I turned 10.

COURAGE ISN'T ABOUT FEARLESSNESS. IT'S TAKING ACTION EVEN THOUGH YOU'RE SCARED.

Always careful about getting value for money, Mum and Dad saw no sense in getting me a small pony I would soon outgrow. Their logic made sense. As I stared up at Roby, 14 hands high, I felt particularly small. However, given that I was now double-digits old, I was determined to make the most of this special birthday present and I set about learning how to ride him.

Every morning before school I'd get up early and head out to the front paddock to catch Roby. A wily old thing, he didn't make it easy on me and I'd often have to enlist the help of my siblings to round him up and put on his bridle. As it so often does, my persistence paid off. By the time I was 11 years old, I was a half competent rider (albeit a rough one) and signing up to compete in the local gymkhana. The problem was, Roby was too slow for the barrel race and no amount of kicking could prod him beyond a sluggish canter. So, before I turned 12, I was back to lobbying my parents — this time for a horse with more 'go'. Call it good luck, the law of attraction or the power of a child's prayer, but just after my twelfth birthday we won a horse in a raffle. Twenty cents a ticket, or six for a dollar. 'The perfect price!' Dad said.

Smokey (ingenuously named because he was the grey colour of smoke!) arrived straight from the rugged mountains of the Victorian high country and had only two speeds: zero and a full gallop. Needless to say, he had more 'go' than Roby. Much more. So I had to dig deep and dial up my courage yet again. Within a few months, and after numerous falls and close scrapes with trees, I'd mastered Smokey and began winning those barrel races. Yee ha!

THE MORE OFTEN YOU ACT BRAVELY, THE MORE YOU GROW YOUR 'MUSCLES FOR LIFE'.

I don't share this story to impress you with my horsemanship. In fact, by the time I was 17 I had largely given up riding because I was too busy finishing my high-school studies and flipping burgers in the nearby village cafe to earn money for university. Rather, I share it because learning to ride Roby, and later Smokey, taught me early on that the more often we act bravely, the braver we become.

Building courage by taking action amid our self-doubts, misgivings and fears is a lesson I've learned many times since leaving my parents' farm — first to study business at university in Melbourne, later backpacking around the globe and starting my first career in the corporate world, and then forging a second career while raising four young children. Time and time again I've discovered that the only way to tame fear is by stepping right through the raw heart of it. By staring down our fear and pursuing challenges that inspire us even as they scare us (like having that fourth child!), we nurture strengths, hone talents and unlock potential that would otherwise have remained dormant.

EVERY WORTHWHILE ENDEAVOUR REQUIRES MAKING YOURSELF VULNERABLE.

As you look back on your life up to now, I'm sure you can recall having to do things that scared you at the time, but which no longer do. Having done them many times, the fear they once incited was replaced with a quiet confidence that flowed into other areas of your life. Bravery (and courage—I use the words synonymously throughout this book) does that. In fact, clinical studies confirm that by practising new behaviours we build and then strengthen neural pathways in our brain so that, over time, they become our unconscious default behaviours. Likewise, when you consciously choose to say and do things outside your comfort zone, you build your 'courage muscles' for taking on bigger challenges and for responding more bravely to those that land unwanted in your lap ... because, sooner or later, they will!

While the lessons and insights I share in the pages to follow are supported by a wealth of psychological research, I had no desire to write an intellectual exploration of risk-taking, the neuro-science of fear or how to overcome it. There are many excellent books written by research psychologists and neuroscientists that do just that. Rather, I wrote *Train the Brave* to help you become more conscious of where fear may be holding the balance of power in your life and to share practical ways for you to reclaim that power so you can make more conscious and courageous choices to truly thrive in your work, relationships and life (no matter what is going on around you!).

TO THRIVE IN OUR CULTURE OF FEAR WE MUST NOT LET IT SET UP RESIDENCE IN OUR LIVES.

Fear is a powerful emotion wired into our psychological DNA to protect us from pain. Yet left unchecked it can infiltrate into every corner of our lives, erode our confidence, amplify our anxiety and steer us down a path of cautious, comfortable — but oh so vanilla — mediocrity. Our culture, and the media that shape it, thrives on fear. Fear sells. Fear wins votes. Fear feeds on itself. Needless to say, at every turn we're bombarded with reasons to feel afraid, play safe, settle and sell out, batten down the hatches, stock up on canned food and buy that Hummer! Yet in our increasingly anxious, accelerated and uncertain world, it's only by discerning the legitimate fears that are serving us from the imagined and sensationalised ones that aren't that we can forge the deeply authentic, meaningful and truthful lives we yearn to live. Only then can we live powerfully, consciously choosing to move towards the aspirations that inspire us, rather than away from the fears that stifle and diminish us.

COURAGE IS A HABIT AND LIKE ALL HABITS, IT CAN BE LEARNED.

Just as the way you fold your arms — right over left or left over right — is something you do without any thought (go on, try it now), so too is how you engage in the world around you. The more often you act a certain way, the more habitual that behaviour becomes, until it's second nature and hard to do any other way. And so it is with living bravely. The more often you 'train the brave' that waits quietly within you, the braver you become. One act of raw courage at a time, one day at a time, over the passage of time *you become what you do*: brave, strong, self-reliant and equipped with everything it takes to pursue your greatest aspirations.

Sir Edmund Hillary, who, along with Tenzing Norgay, was the first man to ascend Mt Everest, did not begin his mountaineering career by taking on the world's tallest mountain. He started by climbing the smaller peaks in his homeland of New Zealand. There, he built up the skill, strength, stamina and courage needed to raise his sights to the most indomitable summit of all. Likewise, as Dr Gordon Livingston wrote, 'If we aspire to be brave we must practice it in small ways so we are prepared when more is required. Because sooner or later, more will be required'.

Turn on the news today and you'll find reports of people who seem hell-bent on inciting fear and oppressing freedom. While we're right to look to our leaders to act with courage, we must first look to ourselves — into our own hearts, homes, workplaces and communities — and ask ourselves, 'Where am I failing to act with the courage I wish to see more of in others?' Only when those of us with the freedom to stand up, to speak up and to champion for change find the courage to do so, can we create a more peaceful, equitable and secure world for those who still don't. Just imagine the world we could create if we each took personal responsibility and all committed to living braver lives driven by what inspired us rather than what scared us.

GROWTH AND COMFORT NEVER RIDE THE SAME HORSE.

Train the Brave is not a book to be read only once, nor does it have to be read in any particular order beyond the first part, which outlines the 10 'building blocks' for living bravely. It's a book to be read with an open heart, an open mind and a pen in your hand. Pick it up whenever you have a moment to yourself, lay your hand on its cover and trust that whatever page falls open holds a message that's beckoning you to greater bravery in some aspect of your life. At the end of each chapter I've given you a short 'Train the Brave' challenge, which invites you to move from 'thinking' to 'doing'. At the end of the book is an invitation to join my *10-day Train the Brave Challenge* to further help you step boldly into action. Nothing beats it!

Growth and comfort never ride the same horse. I learned that growing up on the farm and I've learned it countless times since. Living a deeply meaningful and rewarding life calls on you to step outside your comfort zone — to stretch yourself and to trust yourself — again and again and again. While it's never easy, it's always worthwhile because while bravery won't always guarantee your success — in work, in love and in life — it will always precede it.

Dare bravely. Work bravely. Love bravely. Lead bravely. Live bravely.

Living your life fully — purposefully, passionately and wholeheartedly — is a life-long journey of learning to embrace your vulnerability and accept your fallibility, all the while trusting in yourself that you were born for a mighty purpose and are stronger than anything you ever face. If this book helps you to see this truth more clearly, even in some small way, then it has served its purpose. In doing so, you've helped me to serve mine. For that I'm deeply honoured and immensely grateful.

Part I
Live purposefully

Ten building blocks for living bravely

CHAPTER 1
Decide what you stand for

I was at university at the time of the massacre that took place in China's Tiananmen Square in 1989 — I was the same age as many of those who stood up to the tanks, soldiers and mighty military apparatus of the Chinese government. I remember being in awe of their bravery, particularly that of the young man standing his ground in front of an enormous armoured tank, an image that became iconic when it was broadcast around the globe.

'How could he do that?' I remember asking myself at the time, completely unable to imagine myself being so courageous. And I think it's fair to say, I never have been.

But there are many ways you can be brave. Few make the headlines. Few earn medals. Fewer still make the cover of *Time* magazine. However, every act of bravery stems from a decision to make a stand for something that's bigger than yourself and more important than your emotional safety, comfort or pride.

If you've grown up in a democracy that respects civil liberties and freedom of speech then you've likely never felt compelled to risk your life for the greater good. Consider yourself fortunate. But regardless of your good fortune in life — or lack thereof — we're all called to make a stand for something: for the values we care about, for the difference we want to make, for the causes we believe in and for the injustice we don't. Those of us born with rights and freedoms millions only dream of have an even greater obligation to do so.

WHEN YOU'RE UNCLEAR ABOUT WHAT YOU STAND FOR, YOU CAN FALL EASILY ONTO THE PATH OF CAUTIOUS, COMFORTABLE MEDIOCRITY.

Of course, it's so easy to unintentionally find yourself living on autopilot. We think we're in charge of our thoughts and behaviours, but so often we're operating from habit, reacting unconsciously to perceived threats to our security and station. Fear steers us away from risk and towards safety — or at least the illusion of it. Which is why, unless you're clear about what you want your life to stand for, it's all too easy to fall mindlessly into the path of least resistance, maximum self-interest and minimal contribution. Unfortunately, that path rarely leads anywhere worth travelling. It almost certainly contributes little to the welfare of others, which is always the richest source of satisfaction in our own lives.

Deciding to make a stand for something bigger than yourself is indispensable for living bravely. While you may never be called to lay your life on the line, start a movement or end an unjust regime, every day there are opportunities for you to lay your pride on the line for a more important cause. Sometimes your courage will be rewarded — your risk will pay off, you'll get the job, land the date, win the client, resolve the issue, close the sale, earn the rise. Other times it won't. But who you become by the courage you've shown will always leave you better off. Stronger. Smarter. Braver. Bolder.

KNOWING WHAT YOU STAND FOR IS THE FOUNDATION STONE UPON WHICH BRAVERY IS BUILT.

Each time you make a stand for something you believe in, you make an unspoken, but profoundly important, declaration to those around you — and, most importantly, to yourself:

> ***I'm the author of my life, and not a passive spectator watching life play out before me. My life matters, my voice matters and my choices matter. I will not cower to conformity. I will not surrender to self-doubt. I have a role to play, a difference to make and I'm committed to living my truth, standing for what is right and against what isn't.***

In her book *My Story*, former Australian Prime Minister Julia Gillard wrote that it was her strong sense of purpose that fuelled her determination to enter politics and then sustained her throughout her three turbulent years leading Australia. Upon asking her to share her thoughts for my *Forbes* column to honour International Women's Day the following year, she replied, 'Changing the world, like living your own life well, requires a sense of purpose, the courage to pursue it and the preparedness to risk the most public of failures'. Indeed, Julia ultimately experienced just that. But by having the courage to make a stand for something, she made a far more meaningful impact on her country and the world than she would ever have done otherwise.

Sure, we may not all feel called to enter politics, but there are things that you, and *only* you, can do; things that will never be done if you don't do them. Making a stand for what's most important to you in this one and only precious life of yours requires letting go excuses and owning your power. It means giving up stories that suggest you aren't good enough and daring to believe that you have everything it takes to live a life that truly matters, and to leave a legacy that lasts.

Your life, like my own, is ultimately very short. Knowing what you stand for is your testimony to the world and the only thing that will compel you to step beyond your comfort zone as many times as you need to honour all that you are, all that you can be and the difference that you alone can make.

Train the brave

Knowing what you stand for in your work, in your family and in the world is crucial for living a truly meaningful life. So take a moment to get clear about (or simply to reconnect with) what you want your life to stand for. Write it down (it makes a difference!). Include the impact you want to make on those you live with, work with and encounter throughout the course of your life. Mahatma Ghandi said, 'My life is my message'. What message do you want your life to say between now and the day you die?

CHAPTER 2
Interrogate your reality

A squadron of soldiers was marching through the local town. All the parents and families had come out to wave and cheer them on. One particular soldier was marching completely out of step and as he passed his mother she turned to her neighbour and said, 'Look, my son is the only one marching in step!'

While no-one likes to think they're being as one-eyed as the woman in this parable, all of us can become a victim of our own biases, blinkered thinking, and misperceptions. Left unchallenged, they can shield us from confronting truths we'd prefer not to face and prevent us from taking the very actions needed to forge more meaningful and rewarding lives.

THE STORIES YOU TELL YOURSELF EITHER EXPAND OR SHRINK WHAT'S POSSIBLE FOR YOU. REWRITE THOSE THAT CONFINE YOUR FUTURE.

'Have you ever noticed that anybody driving slower than you is an idiot, and anyone going faster than you is a maniac?' This question by comedian George Carlin observes the bias we all have in assuming that our perception of reality is the right one and that everyone else has got it wrong. The truth is that you don't see the world as it is; you see it as you are. The reality you live in is shaped not by the circumstances of your life, but by the lens through which you view them and the story you create. In turn, what you tell yourself is the 'truth' impacts the emotions you feel, the actions you take and the outcomes you produce ... for better or worse. Every story you have either expands what's possible for you, or it shrinks it. So while the stories you tell yourself are often far from reality, they ultimately shape it.

WHATEVER YOU TELL YOURSELF IS TRUE, YOUR BRAIN AUTOMATICALLY GOES TO WORK TO PROVE YOURSELF RIGHT.

For most of my life I had labeled myself an 'unathletic non-runner' and created a convincing story (convincing to me at least) about how my legs just weren't made for running. Then a few years ago I joined a boot camp and found myself running. Slowly. Heavily. But running nonetheless. Week by week, as my fitness improved, it chipped away at my well entrenched 'I can't run' story. Then I signed up for a 5k run. Then a 10k. Then a 15k. Then a half-marathon. After I finished the half-marathon my mum said to me, 'When you were fourteen you would have said running 21 kilometres (13 miles) was a physical impossibility.' Indeed, I would have! Which just goes to show how profoundly the stories we tell ourselves can shape (and limit!) what we even attempt to accomplish.

We all have a lot vested in our view of the world and we all get some sort of payoff by sticking to it — whether it be a sense of righteousness or victimhood, or an excuse for avoiding the pain and discomfort of facing the sometimes difficult and harsh realities of our lives. Or of simply doing the hard work required to make a change! It's why we tend to become defensive when anyone challenges how we see things, including how we see ourselves. In fact, psychologists have found that we actively ignore or discredit information that flies in the face of our own views (what they call our 'perceptual defence mechanism') and we actively seek out information that supports it ('confirmation bias'). If you've ever had to deal with a parent who thinks their child is the brightest or most gifted on the planet — when in fact their child is a little brat — you've encountered both.

BECAUSE YOU'RE HARDWIRED TO DEFEND YOUR VIEW OF REALITY, YOU MUST CONTINUALLY QUESTION IT.

We're instinctively drawn to information that reinforces what we already believe or hope. Whatever you decide about a situation, person or yourself — good, bad or impossible — your mind automatically goes to work to prove that you're right. Which is why you need to push yourself to actively seek out information that can jar your view of the world — something you're wired to avoid doing! Yet it's the information that challenges your existing paradigms, stories, assumptions (like being unable to run!) and beliefs that yields the most valuable insights and results.

Of course, it takes courage to acknowledge the possibility that the way you've always seen something — such as a situation, person, group or organisation — may in fact be wrong. It takes even more courage to open yourself up to rewriting a new story and approaching it in a new way. It's why so many people go to their grave holding onto beliefs that have left them lonely, angry or unhappy. They were never brave enough to admit that maybe *they* had it wrong (and not everyone else); or that the opportunities they never got were because they never had the courage to seek or seize them.

UNCHALLENGED PERCEPTIONS ARE RARELY REALITY, BUT THEY HOLD THE POWER TO SHAPE IT.

Any area of your life in which you feel anything from mild dissatisfaction through to deep resentment or unhappiness is an area in which your 'story' of reality may benefit from a little (or a lot) of interrogation and then some rewriting. You can start by asking yourself these questions, and being brutally honest in your answers:

» Does my current story about this situation/person expand or shrink possibilities? (If you're using negative labels such as 'I'm hopeless' or absolute words such as 'I can never', 'They always' or 'It's impossible', it's likely to be shrinking them!)

» What evidence can I find that contradicts my story of reality? (For example, are there other people in similar circumstances doing things I say can't be done?)

» Where have I cast people as villains, or myself as a 'victim', in ways that make me feel powerless and incapable of creating the change I want?

» What other story could I tell about this situation that would shift negative emotions and open up more possibilities for action? (Write it down!)

» What payoff would I need to give up, if I changed my current story, that could be fuelling my resistance to change? (For example, we all get a payoff from our sense of victimhood or righteousness.)

THE MAP IS NOT THE TERRITORY.

John Lennon once said, 'Reality leaves a lot to the imagination.' Likewise, just as a map of a place doesn't reflect the actual terrain when you arrive there, so too your mental map of reality is not a pure reflection of it. If you don't like where your current map has landed you, then perhaps it's because it's either out of date or it was inaccurate to begin with. Either way, it needs to go the way of the Dodo. Just like an old map, your stories about yourself, others and the world you live in each day either expand your possibilities or they shrink them; they either infuse your life with greater joy and meaning, or they deplete it. If you don't like the results you're getting, then take a step back and interrogate your reality. Like me, you may even end up doing something you once believed was impossible!

Train the brave

Think of an area in your life where you've had an ongoing sense of dissatisfaction. Now, being brutally honest with yourself, consider how your story and perceptions about it may have been limiting how constructively you've dealt with it, or even exacerbated it. How could you rewrite that story, which has caused you to feel unhappy, hurt, powerless or afraid, in a way that opens up new possibilities for dealing with it more courageously and successfully?

CHAPTER 3

Face your fear to rise above it

When I asked my son Ben what he wanted for his thirteenth birthday he pondered the question for about 10 seconds before replying, 'To go sky diving'. While I was a bit taken aback, given that Andrew and I had both gone parachuting in our 'pre-kids' days, I knew it would be hypocritical to say it was too dangerous. Not only would Ben be doing a tandem jump attached to a professional sky-diver (whereas Andrew and I had jumped solo our first time), but statistically I knew that there was more chance of us being killed in a car crash on the way to the plane than of him being hurt jumping out of it. So I parked my fears and focused on the excitement that lay in store for him.

On 'jump morning', as I was driving him to the drop-off point to sign 101 waiver forms and meet the professional diver he'd be strapped to, I asked Ben if he was nervous.

'Nah, not much. Should I be?'

'Nope,' I said, biting my tongue (because I remembered being teeth-chatteringly terrified the time I jumped out of a plane!) and trying to redirect my now wandering imagination from thinking about a failed chute.

An hour later, I sat on the side of the grassy landing field, staring up into the cloudless blue sky, searching for his small plane to make an appearance overhead. Soon after I spotted it I could see a tiny black dot coming out of it. That was my Ben! I then waited to see his chute deploy. Each second felt like an eternity. But then *Wallah!*—out it came and I watched with delight (and relief!) as he glided back down to earth, landing safely nearby.

With his blue eyes wide and a broad smile beaming off his face, the first words out of his mouth said it all. 'That was absolutely fantasmagorical, Mum. I want the exact same thing for my fourteenth birthday!'

We'll see!

NOTHING CAN ROB OUR FREEDOM MORE QUICKLY THAN FEAR.

Ben later shared that he had (like his mother before him) felt absolutely terrified while he sat at the open doorway of the small plane just before jumping (he is—after all—human!). Yet his relative lack of anxiety brought home the reality of fear; that is, fear is a product of the thoughts we create, a projection of some future occurrence and often something that has *yet* to happen—something that may be unlikely to *ever* happen. Yet our imaginations can amplify the odds exponentially and leave us paralysed with fear.

It's not the event or object we fear that holds power over us; it's our fear of it. Left unchecked, fear can set up permanent residence in our lives and keep us stuck in one place with the grip of a vice. The more we relent, the harder it is to free ourselves. It's why so many people live their lives held hostage to fear, never doing what they truly want or knowing who they truly are. As J. Ruth Gendler wrote, 'Fear has a large shadow, but he himself is small'.

Of course, we shouldn't cast fear as the 'bad guy' we want to permanently eradicate from our lives. It's not. Like all emotions, it's wired into our psychic DNA for a reason: to protect us from danger and alert us to potential threats to our safety. This is why, in a culture of fear, we have to be increasingly discerning about the fears we buy into, vigilant about not letting others' fears become our own and mindful of the ubiquitous nature of fear, which can keep us living on the sidelines — in the shadows — instead of taking the leading role in our own lives.

MOST PEOPLE SUFFER FAR MORE FROM THEIR IMAGINATION THAN THEY EVER DO FROM THEIR REALITY.

'I am an old man and have known a great many troubles, but most of them have never happened.' These words, penned by Mark Twain in his final years, observe the irony that most of the things we spend our lives afraid of never actually happen. Our plane doesn't crash. Our children don't get abducted. We don't contract lethal viruses. The thing you fear may happen is not what holds power over you, it's your fear of how you will feel if the worst eventuates. The sad irony is that in people's efforts to avoid such (usually remote) possibilities they inadvertently create more angst, more heartache and more hardship for themselves than they would have created had they been courageous enough to risk outright exposure. They also fail to build the self-efficacy, resiliency and 'courage muscles' to rise above the storm waves when they inevitably roll in.

IT'S NOT WHAT YOU THINK YOU FEAR, IT'S WHAT YOU LINK TO FEAR.

I once read that we tend to be afraid of our feelings for the same reason we're afraid of ghosts: we can't see them, we can't catch them and we can't control them. Consequently, we go through life with a 'feeling phobia', afraid to feel fully and confusing what it is we think we fear with what we link to fear.

You *think* you are scared of the dark. You're *really* scared of what may be in it.

You *think* you're afraid of heights. You're *really* afraid of falling to the ground.

You *think* you're afraid of losing money. You're *really* afraid of feeling worthless.

You *think* you're afraid of commitment. You're *really* afraid of being hurt.

You *think* you're afraid of hurting someone. You're *really* afraid of how *you'll* feel if you do.

You *think* you're afraid of parting ways. You're *really* just afraid you'll be alone.

WHEN YOU ACKNOWLEDGE YOUR FEARS, YOU DILUTE THEIR STRENGTH.

Only by exposing fear to the truth can you dilute its strength and loosen its grip. What opens up in the place that fear once occupied is a whole new sense of freedom, and with it, possibility—freedom to live authentically, to speak truthfully, to pursue your most audacious dreams, and to step away from the naysayers and towards a new future, however uncertain.

By asking yourself what's the worst thing you fear may happen and then sitting in the place of it happening, you come to know that even if it did happen—which is unlikely—it wouldn't kill you. Rather, you'd reveal yourself to you.

WHEN YOU TAKE ACTION DESPITE YOUR FEAR YOU DIMINISH ITS POWER AND AMPLIFY YOUR OWN.

You build your own brand of brave every time you consciously choose to move towards what inspires you, rather than away from what scares you. Whether it's something small such as inviting people over for dinner or introducing yourself to someone you look up to, asking your boss for support or confiding a struggle to a friend. Or whether it's something bigger, such as leaving your secure job to go out on your own, having another baby, moving abroad or acknowledging a broken marriage.

The more you face your fear, stare it down and then step right through the heart of it, the more you strengthen your faith in yourself and your courage for life. It's why I encourage my children to do what inspires them, even if it scares them (and me!). Acting bravely in small ways when it doesn't seem to matter so much is what enables you to build your courage for when it does. You begin by asking yourself, 'What would I do if I weren't afraid?', and then trusting yourself that whatever direction your answer beckons, you have all the courage you need to travel there.

Train the brave

What would you do today, this month or this year if you were being truly courageous? What fears would you need to overcome to do it? Acknowledging what you're afraid of is the first step to taming your fear. So identify exactly what it is you're so afraid of. Then imagine your worst fear coming through and breathe deeply into it. Imagine yourself in the midst of that situation feeling strong and

(continued)

Train the brave *(cont'd)*

secure in yourself. How would you handle it? What would you learn about yourself in the process?

The purpose of this exercise isn't to feed your fear but to help you realise that it's not the event you fear may happen that's holding you back, it's the fear you've got around it. Fear itself can't hurt you. By consciously choosing to take action in its presence you diminish its power and discover your own. If you don't believe me, just try it.

CHAPTER 4
Value your own opinion above all others

Around the time my mum and dad had their seventh child (my sister Cath), they realised they needed to trade in their Kingswood station wagon for something bigger. Dad managed to track down an old plumber's van that was going at a price he could afford. He then installed windows in the back, three rows of bench seats and handcrafted his very own drop-down coffee table. It was fair to say we had a one-of-a-kind family van!

While Dad was rightly proud of his handy work, I was highly self-conscious, wishing we had a 'normal' car like everyone else. When we drove into the nearby town of Bairnsdale, about half an hour away, I'd duck down out of public view whenever we were in Main Street to avoid being seen by anyone, particularly kids from my school or boys from the local footy club. I used to tell my parents to let me know when it was safe to sit up again. Yet I lost count of the times my dad would tell me that the coast was clear and I'd raise my head in perfect time to see a bunch of kids from my school staring right at me. Dad would chuckle to himself as I dived back for cover admonishing him with, 'Dad, what will everybody think?!'

IF YOU DON'T APPROVE OF YOURSELF, NO AMOUNT OF PRAISE WILL EVER BE ENOUGH.

Of course, most teenagers are desperate to fit into the pack and avoid anything that makes them look different. But while my self-consciousness may have been normal teenage behaviour, most of us carry our desire for external approval and 'looking good' with us well into adulthood. The truth is that if you aren't able to approve of yourself first, no amount of adulation, admiration or approval from anyone else will be enough. *Ever.*

THOSE WHO JUDGE HARSHLY DO SO FROM THEIR OWN FEAR OF INADEQUACY.

Of course, as human beings we're hardwired to want to belong to a tribe. It's natural to want to be liked, admired and thought well of by those whose opinions we value. Yet unless we're conscious about what's driving us, we can easily fall into the trap of living our lives on autopilot, driven to act, dress, say and do whatever it takes to avoid being criticised, disliked or rejected and to secure our place in whatever tribe we aspire to belong to. Without being consciously aware of it, we can grow more attached to what others think of us — or what we *think* they think — than what we think of ourselves. In doing so, we surrender our power to the opinion of others and we let them play us small.

'What will everybody think?' is a question I've heard many people ask in many contexts across a spectrum from the most mundane to the most significant. What will everyone think of my outfit? What will everyone think of me ending my marriage? What will everyone think of me quitting my job, or starting a business, or being open about my sexuality? The funny thing is that psychologists have found that, for most people, our 'everybody' consists of about five or six people. That is, we aren't concerned about what 'everyone' in the world will think; we're worried about what a few key people will think. But regardless of who makes up your 'everybody', the only worthy answer to the question 'What will everybody think?' is this:

So what?!

While some of the people we want approval from may be those whose opinions we respect, too often they're people driven by their own fears and insecurities. Bending yourself inside out to appease the naysayers in your life will leave you not only playing small, but on a sure course to resentment, regret or both. Because no matter what you do there will be some people who will find fault with it. That's not because you're not good enough; it's because they're afraid they're not. As Marianne Williamson wrote, 'There is nothing enlightened about shrinking so that other people will not feel insecure around you'.

YOU'D CARE LESS ABOUT WHAT 'EVERYBODY' THINKS OF YOU IF YOU KNEW HOW SELDOM THEY DO.

Not only is your 'everybody' a few billion people less than 'every body', but research shows that we assume 'everybody' even cares about what we're doing. In fact, studies have found that we assume we're getting about twice as much attention as we really are. So while you're sweating it out thinking that everyone is talking about you and critiquing your actions, they're actually absorbed in worrying about what people are thinking of them! In fact, chances are you've hardly made a blip on their radar. The 'spotlight' effect — as it's been called — shows people usually pay about fifty per cent as much attention to you as you think they do. Needless to say, it can be an oppressive force. The irony is that if you did everything twice as bravely and spoke up twice as boldly, you wouldn't attract any more attention than you do right now. However, you'd probably feel a whole lot better about yourself if you did.

YOU RELINQUISH YOUR POWER TO PEOPLE EVERY TIME YOU LET THEIR OPINIONS DICTATE YOUR ACTIONS.

When you allow what other people think to determine your actions — whether it's what you'll say or wear, where you send your kids to school, go to church, the lifestyle you live or who you aspire to become — you surrender your power and hand it over to other people who may have very different values, perceptions and preferences from you. In short, when you let what other people think determine what you'll say or do — or who you'll become — you're essentially giving those people the power to run your life. Needless to say, it's a very powerless way to live.

While you may always care about others thinking well of you, by becoming conscious of the times when you're giving other people's opinions too much power, you can liberate yourself to forge a path that's much more rewarding, less exhausting and immeasurably more authentic. And the irony is that the less you care about what others think of you, the more they actually will.

Letting your fear of what everybody may be thinking of you magnify your self-consciousness, keeps you from expressing yourself authentically and living truthfully. Just imagine how much more liberated you'd feel if you no longer cared about what everybody thought about you. What new possibilities would open up for you if you let go of your need for others to like you and were willing to risk criticism or disapproval? As Cher once said, 'Until you're ready to look foolish, you will never have the possibility of being great'.

My siblings and I often share fond memories about our road trips in the the old van. Like the time it broke down on the main road in front of my high school and a bunch of boys had to be pulled from PE class on the adjacent field to push-start it while my year-8 geography class watched, laughing, from a window. ('Isn't that your car Margie?') I wanted to dig a deep, *deep* hole and bury myself in it. In hindsight, I wish I'd had the confidence back then to care less and laugh more. While I'd love to tell you I don't give a second thought to what people may think of me, I can't. But I've become better at not letting what people may think occupy the driver's seat. Whether it's driving a converted plumber's van or driving your life, when fear of what 'everybody' thinks is steering your choices and directing your life, it will stop you from ever arriving at the place you want to be.

Approve of yourself. Accept yourself. Own your worth. Practise daily and you'll gradually come to realise that you never needed approval from anyone else to feel whole and happy. Only from yourself.

Train the brave

How would letting go of your concern of what others think free you to express yourself more authentically? What would you do differently if you didn't care what others may say or think?

CHAPTER 5
Trust your intuition

An odd feeling in your gut. A subtle sense of foreboding. A funny inkling. A knowing whisper: 'This just *feels* right' . Or wrong.

I'm sure you've felt those intuitive murmurs before. The question is, how often have you trusted them? And those times you didn't, how did it cost you — professionally, personally, financially or physically?

Beyond our conscious awareness, our 'sixth sense' reads miniscule signals that point us to pay attention to something ... or someone. Wired only to perception, our intuition can guide us to making snap decisions we later marvel at. 'Somehow I just knew,' people will later say about a hidden danger they simply knew to veer away from or an opportunity they spontaneously seized despite knowing little about it.

When I was 21 I set off around the world with little more than a backpack, some traveller's cheques, and a sense of adventure. Along the way I met thousands of people and developed a keen sixth sense about those I could trust and those it was better to steer away from. I remember meeting an off-duty Amtrak conductor, Peter, on an Amtrak train from St Petersburg to Miami. After Peter had told me that the Amtrak station in Miami was miles from the South Beach hostel where I was meeting up with my friend Mia and that the public bus schedule on Sundays was very limited, he offered to give me a lift in his car, which was parked at the station. Accepting his offer would save me either a hefty cab fare or many hours on public buses. Both things I was keen to avoid.

While I'm sure many parents would have been mortified by the idea of their 21-year-old daughter getting a lift with a man she'd just met, I just knew Peter was genuinely trying to help me out of a bind. My intuition proved correct. As he dropped me off at the hostel, he told me that while he was glad I'd accepted his offer to help, I really shouldn't have and that I needed to be less trusting of strangers in the future. I thanked him and promised I'd be careful.

In the years that followed, as I travelled further across Europe, Africa, the Middle East, South America and Asia, I met many other equally generous and genuine people, all the while relying heavily on my gut instinct. I also met a few that I didn't sense were so well intentioned and always gave them a wide berth. Not once did my intuition let me down during my intrepid backpacking days and not once has it given me a bum steer since. The only times I've ever got myself in a difficult situation — whether personally or professionally — was when I was either too busy to listen to my intuition, or I simply ignored it.

FEAR CAN CLOUD YOUR ABILITY TO DISCERN REAL THREATS FROM IMAGINED ONES.

Before you start sending me messages to point out my foolhardiness (or sheer good luck), let me say that I'm well aware that there are risks involved in trusting strangers. But too often today I meet people — young and old alike — who've been so thoroughly conditioned by their environment (including well-intentioned but overly protective parents) to fear every strange person or unfamiliar situation that they can no longer discern between genuine threats to their safety and those merely in their imagination. I've seen far too many people extend trust to people who didn't deserve it while withholding trust from those who did because they didn't listen to their gut.

Gavin De Becker wrote in *The Gift of Fear*, 'Genuine fear is intended to be brief, not to hang around for a long period of time'. So many people live in a constant state of low-grade anxiety, walking through life forever on high alert for danger — killer viruses, catastrophes or predatory people — that they have little capacity left to pick up the subtle signals their intuition may be feeding them about their environment. Of course, the sad irony is that their constant fear doesn't make them safer and more secure; it makes them less so.

Chronic fear diminishes our capacity to tune into our intuition. In turn, it undermines our ability to accurately gauge risk, assess people, develop business acumen, tune into our bodies, render help when needed and perform at our peak. Needless to say, it takes courage both to tune into your intuition and then to trust what it's telling you. However, the more often you do, the more it can guide you.

Founder of *The Huffington Post* Arianna Huffington said that it was only after she began to meditate regularly (a prime way to connect with your intuition) that she was able to dial into intuition fully. It gave her clarity about what she needed to do in her business, which included taking *The Huffington Post* global against the advice of some trusted advisers. It turned out to be an excellent business decision, with more than 50 per cent of her readers now outside the United States.

BE CAREFUL YOUR HEAD DOESN'T HIJACK YOUR HEART.

Deep down you know you have the ability to accomplish something very special to you. And while your head may be arguing with me right now, your heart knows it's true. Far too often I've seen incredibly capable talented people baulk at taking a step forward toward their dreams for fear they don't have what it takes to achieve them. Elite athletes who choke are a great example of people who've trained and prepared and have all the skills, but instead of going into a state of flow, they go into their heads, miss the shot or freeze entirely. So if you've been dreaming of doing something, if you've prepared yourself for it, park the doubt, trust your gut and go for it. Steve Jobs said, 'Have the courage to follow your heart and intuition. They somehow already know what you truly want to become. Everything else is secondary'.

LISTEN TO YOUR BODY. IT DESERVES YOUR ATTENTION.

Most gut instincts are accompanied by some kind of physical sensation, from goose bumps to a tightening in your chest. Sometimes they give you early warning signs that something is amiss in your body. Never ignore them. *Ever.* I've heard far too many sad stories of people who kept ignoring some nagging feeling that all was not well, dismissing it as 'just a bump' or 'just a niggle' until it was too late. I'm sure you have also. Your body is a powerful and intuitive communicator, so tune into it often.

IF IT DOESN'T FEEL RIGHT, IT PROBABLY ISN'T. IF IT DOES, IT PROBABLY IS. YOUR GUT RARELY LIES.

You were born with an inbuilt radar whose purpose is to alert you to people and places that could put you in harm's way. It can give you an 'off' feeling in the company of someone who's just not good for you, whether they have bad intentions or will simply steer you away from fulfilling your biggest purpose. Every time I've entered into a business relationship with the wrong person (fortunately not that often), I can look back and recall having a dodgy feeling about them that I dismissed in my eagerness to believe their promises and later to extend the benefit of the doubt well past its use-by date.

NEVER LET FEAR OF MAKING A WRONG DECISION KEEP YOU FROM MAKING A RIGHT ONE.

Studies have found that the longer people mull over big decisions, the less satisfied they are afterwards than they would have been had they spent less time deciding and simply 'gone with their gut'. So while it's counter-intuitive, when it comes to those big decisions — who to marry, which house to buy, whether to take the job or change career — the less you analyse the pros and cons, the more likely it is that you'll make a decision you're happy with in the long term. Your risk-averse, rational mind can lead you to overthink, over-analyse and make poorer decisions than if you just follow your intuition and do what feels right. Indeed, fear of making a wrong decision can keep you from making a right one!

IF YOU SENSE THAT SOMEONE NEEDS YOUR HELP, JUST GIVE IT.

While gut instincts have evolved to help us avoid danger, we human beings have an equally powerful capacity to sense when others need our help. Compassion, like fear, is one of our most primal emotions, giving us the ability to read faces and pick up unspoken emotional cues. So, if you sense someone needs your help in some way, don't hold back for fear of looking foolish, over-stepping a boundary or risking offence. Too often people do.

It takes courage to put aside your spreadsheets, stop re-running the numbers, and lean into your intuition to guide you forward. But, as Gary Klein — a psychologist who has devoted years to studying intuition — wrote, 'The longer we wait to defend our intuitions, the less we will have to defend'.

Train the brave

Take two minutes right now to close your eyes, follow your breath and just sit with the question, 'What does my intuition want me to know right now?' Perhaps it's a decision you've been struggling with. Perhaps it's how best to approach a situation you've been unsure about. Perhaps it's a prod to do or say something you've been wavering about. Just stop with all your busyness, and get quiet enough that you can hear it. If you don't get any clear inkling right away, that's okay. Simply by giving yourself time to tune into your intuition you'll be more open to the messages it sends your way later today, as you sleep tonight and in the weeks ahead. All that truly matters is that you are open to hearing it and that you have the courage to act on it.

CHAPTER 6
Focus on what you want

At the tender age of 16 my oldest son Lachlan left home, moving from Melbourne, Australia, to Washington DC in the United States (where he'd lived from age 7 to 14) to finish high school. Crazy passionate about basketball, he felt that doing so would put him in a much better place to play college basketball, a burning ambition he'd had for years. My husband and I felt it was important to support him despite the many time zones and 24 hours of air travel that would separate us.

As the countdown to his departure drew nearer, I became more and more torn. He was so young. It was so far (16 000 kilometres away!). His leaving the family nest would create such a huge hole in our daily life ... in my life! Increasingly, I found myself in tears at the very thought of him going away.

My dear friend Graeme was insightful, caring and courageous enough to point out to me that I seemed to be focusing far more on what our family was losing than on all that Lachlan would gain. His words made me realise that

I'd been amplifying my own unhappiness and—albeit unintentionally—diminishing the quality of the time I still had with Lachlan at home.

WHAT YOU FOCUS ON EXPANDS.

Whatever we place our focus on is expanded in our reality ... for better or worse. By dwelling on what I'd lose rather than all that Lachlan had to gain I'd dug myself into an emotional hole that was filled with all my complaints about what I didn't want, rather than my intentions about what I did want. It left me feeling increasingly sad and upset and cut me off from being able to celebrate the brave, big-hearted and thoughtful young man Lachlan had become. Shifting where I was placing my attention didn't negate the grief I felt at his leaving, but it helped me to ride its wave with more gratitude and joy. What a precious gift that was at a time when so many conflicting emotions ran so high.

ENERGY FLOWS WHERE ATTENTION GOES. DON'T BE AN ACCOMPLICE IN YOUR OWN MISERY.

Focusing on what you do want, not on what you don't, isn't about white-washing those aspects of your life that require attention. Nor is it about denying valid emotions such as the sadness that accompanies loss or the anger that rises when you experience injustice. Rather, I'm talking about not being complicit in your own misery by dwelling too much on what pulls you down and too little on what can lift you up.

Your experience of reality is simply a reflection of where you place your attention. This includes the types of conversations you have with others—whether they're focused on what you're grateful about and aspire to achieve, or whether they're spent complaining about what you don't have, don't want and can't do. Either way, if you don't like what you're getting back from the world around you, it will pay you to look at what you're putting out.

THE WORLD IS YOUR MIRROR. IT'S REFLECTING BACK WHAT YOU'RE PUTTING OUT.

Psychologist Albert Bandurra found that when we focus our attention on negative things that make us feel afraid or down on ourselves, it triggers us to recall related memories that reinforce and amplify those emotions in other unrelated areas of our life. So, focusing on things that make you feel afraid only makes you more afraid. Focusing on things that make you feel like a helpless victim only disempowers you further. Focusing on old wounds and hurts only sows more bitterness.

On the flip side, placing your attention on things that make you happy makes you happier. And placing it on things that make you feel confident, inspired and brave will ready you to act in ways that only reinforce those same emotions. In Abraham Lincoln's words, 'Most folks are as happy as they make up their minds to be'. Make up your mind.

So, if there's an aspect of your life that's causing you angst, misery or frustration, or that's simply siphoning your daily joy, ask yourself where you're focusing too much on what you *can't* do or what *isn't* right, rather than on what you can do and what *is* right. Consciously shifting your attention, conversations and efforts not only makes you feel stronger — in body, mind and spirit — but it expands your capacity to handle your challenges and pursue your goals more courageously.

Shifting my focus about Lachlan leaving us for boarding school to pursue his burning passion and ambitions enabled me to make the most of the time I did have with him, and to be a better mum for my remaining three children still living at home. It also helped deepen my gratitude for the fact that he was now making his own brave way towards blossoming into the fullness of the person he was created to be. Truly, what more can any mother ever want?

WHAT YOU THINK, YOU BECOME.

Over the course of your life you will find that what you focus on will come to you. So hold in your mind whatever you want more of. What you focus on, you create. What you think about, you become.

Train the brave

Where can you focus more of your attention on what you want more of? How can you shift the focus of your conversations to be less about what you *don't* want and more about what you *do* want? Try doing this today and notice how it shifts your energy and upgrades your reality.

CHAPTER 7

Own your choices; spare the excuses

'I'm too old to change career now,' Tony lamented to me. He'd always worked in accounting and had been quite successful, but he'd long ago lost his passion for it and was struggling with the future ahead of him. 'I always wanted to be a high-school maths teacher, but if I go back now to qualify as a teacher I'll be 51 before I get into a classroom.'

There was no arguing with his arithmetic. He would be 51. But, as I pointed out to him, he was also the youngest age he'd be for the rest of his life and he could spend the next 20-plus years wishing he'd just taken the plunge.

Then there's Kerrie, who stayed in her marriage for all the wrong reasons — financial security, social status, fear of being alone — and then, 25 years later, found herself feeling very lonely, starved for intimacy, betrayed by infidelity, and regretting that she hadn't had the courage to step out and start over years — decades! — earlier.

Too old. Too young. Too busy.

Not connected enough. Not experienced enough. Not clever enough.

OUR LIVES ARE SHAPED BY THE QUALITY OF OUR CHOICES, TOO OFTEN DISGUISED AS EXCUSES.

Let's face it, you will always—*always*—be able to find a multitude of convenient reasons to explain why your life is not as you want it to be, and why now isn't the right time to change what you don't want or pursue what you do.

Of course, there's always some validity to excuses. You *do* have a lot on. You aren't as young as you once were. You aren't as experienced as you'd like. You don't know exactly what you're doing. You aren't as connected as you want. You would have to drop your salary, give up your office and put your reputation on the line. Heck, you may even fail! And yes, you *could* also spend another year getting more qualified, more prepared, more organised. You *could* spend another decade getting the experience or building the connections or confidence you'd like, too. You could do a lot of things! But at what cost?

YOU CAN ALWAYS FIND REASONS TO JUSTIFY YOUR LOT IN LIFE AND WHY YOU AREN'T ABLE TO IMPROVE IT.

You will always find plenty of people to support your reasons, justify your caution and affirm your inaction. I always have! But they've never been the people I admire most: the doers, the go-getters and the trailblazers. That's because truly successful people don't trade in excuses, which, if you're really honest about it, are just convenient lies you tell yourself to cover up the fact that you either don't want to do something (which is fine—but then just say so and own it!) or you're afraid you'll fail if you try.

If you want to live bravely, you have to stop making excuses for your life and start owning your choices. *Every single one of them.* From the choice to put that chocolate chip muffin in your mouth to the choice to not share how hurt you feel.

Living bravely means living powerfully from choice. So be very conscious in the choices you're making and clear about why you're making them. If you've continually made excuses about why you can't change what you aren't happy with, take a step back and ask yourself how committed you truly are. Perhaps you're just not willing to put in the effort or take the risk or make the sacrifice, like my friend Tony (he's still in accounting, just playing more golf). If so, own it. Or maybe you're simply afraid that if you try you'll fail. In which case, own that too and then, very consciously, decide if you're okay with letting your fear of failure be the deciding factor. If you are okay, that's fine. But own it and own it fully and stop making excuses for it.

I've always valued the friends in my life who have countered my excuses with things like 'That's just a hurdle, not a permanent obstacle', or 'So what? You'll figure it out!'. While a part of me squirms at the faith they have in me, the biggest part of me cheers, 'Yes, that's exactly right. One way or another, I *will* figure it out'. Like when I decided to begin a new career as a coach with four children under the age of six. I was extremely busy. There was the possibility we'd be relocated with my husband's job. I had minimal experience and even fewer connections (we'd moved to the United States two years earlier). Coaching was an increasingly crowded market with low entry barriers (it felt like every second person I met was becoming a 'life coach' at the time) and I didn't quite know what I was doing. But I was passionate and I was committed. And so, while there were plenty of convenient excuses not to bother trying, I knew that if I gave those excuses power I'd look back and wonder, 'What if?' So try I did. And while the path has been neither smooth nor straight (and I've since moved house/state/hemisphere four times!), it's been one of the most rewarding adventures of my life.

It's all too easy to lay blame and abdicate responsibility for the shape of our relationships, health, careers, happiness and lives. It's why so many of us do just that. It's why many — too many — live in the shadow of their excuses rather than owning the choices that have them living as they do, where they do, how they do ... for better or worse. In the end, their excuses shape their lives.

A YEAR FROM NOW YOU'LL WISH YOU STARTED TODAY.

Florence Nightingale once said, 'I attribute my success to this: I never gave or took any excuse'. Likewise, I encourage you to park your excuses whenever they keep you living small and safe and stuck. Don't wait for the stars, the moon and the planets to align before you take action towards whatever it is that tugs at your heart or drags it down. Don't wait to become a 'morning person'. Don't wait to get more experience. Don't wait to get your parents' blessing. Don't wait to pay off your mortgage. Don't wait until the kids leave home. Don't wait to become a master of your trade. Instead, start owning every choice you make; own the consequences of them, and own the possibilities they open up or close down. Just don't hide behind excuses and justifications. You're better than that and you know it.

LIVING BRAVELY REQUIRES LIVING POWERFULLY FROM CHOICE.

Living bravely means deciding to be bigger than the excuses you've rested on up to now, and owning the impact every choice you've ever made has had on where you are now and on the future you are heading into. Having the courage to take complete responsibility for your life can fundamentally transform your experience of being alive. Whether you're 21 or 61. Whether you're a PhD or never finished high school. Whether you have three young children or 23 grandchildren. It doesn't matter.

If taking personal responsibility for our lives — our health, finances, careers, relationships, family harmony and the physical environment we inhabit — was easy to do, we'd live in a vastly different world. The truth is that it takes courage to look in the mirror and own your life. But only when you take full ownership of your life can you reclaim the power you've been giving to those excuses, complaints and justifications and move yourself back into the driver's seat.

YOU CREATE YOUR OWN DESTINY, ONE CHOICE AT A TIME. MAKE BRAVE ONES.

Truly successful people are the least inclined to make excuses. They don't hold power and influence because it's been given to them, but because of how they've used the power they've always had. The same power resides in you. So, whatever it is that is not as you'd like it right now, don't make excuses for why it is as it is and why you can't do anything about it. Rather, get up from your seat, roll up your sleeves and make things happen!

The biggest barrier you face to achieving what you want is not in all the reasons you have about why it's so difficult to achieve, but in making a commitment to overcoming the obstacles, owning your choices and sparing the excuses. Only you get to decide how you'll show up each day, who you'll be, what you'll do and the attitude you'll bring to your life.

Your life is the lump sum of all your choices. Don't run the risk of looking back 10 years from now and realising that all those excuses you had were simply that — excuses. And not even particularly good ones. Be bolder than your best excuses. Own your choices. Only when you take full responsibility for the life you've created until now can you be powerful in creating the life you want from here on.

Train the brave

Where have you been choosing to make excuses for not addressing those aspects of your life that don't make you feel great about yourself and your future? How are they costing you? What new choices are you ready to make? Make one today. Repeat again tomorrow. I promise you, each powerful choice you make today amplifies your ability to make bigger and better ones tomorrow.

CHAPTER 8

Resist conformity; embrace what makes you different

Carly Findlay has spent her entire life looking different from most people. Born with a rare skin condition called ichthyosis, her skin is constantly shedding its outer layer, making it highly sensitive to the sunlight and outdoors. Her condition also means she has no eyebrows or eyelashes and causes her skin to look very red, intensified by the thick, shiny cream she has to apply when she goes outdoors. Needless to say, Carly has never looked like what society would consider 'normal' and she never will. But as Carly said when we first met to film one of my 'conversations of courage' interviews, 'Why would I want to?!'

From the outset, I was struck by how accepting Carly was about her appearance, and even more so, by how powerful she was because of it. During our conversation, Carly shared that while she used to be self-conscious during her teen years, she gradually shifted how she saw her condition from something to be embarrassed about to something to embrace with pride. 'This is who I am; it doesn't make me weird; it makes me special. Sure some people look at me and turn away, but that is their problem, not mine.' It's no surprise that Carly has become an international advocate for people who look visibly different, inspiring others to embrace their appearance rather than to hide it.

WHAT A SHAME TO MAKE YOURSELF BORING BY DIALLING DOWN WHAT MAKES YOU UNIQUE.

Of course, not all of us have physical differences that make us stand out, but how many people do you know who spend enormous amounts of time, money and energy trying to get their body to conform to the ideal shape? And how many people do you 'sort of' know ... but not really? Over the years I've encountered many people who, in their effort to climb the social or corporate ladder, have dialled down those aspects about themselves that could make them stand out or garner criticism. In the process they've disconnected from those parts of themselves that make them interesting and unique. Some people wear a mask for so long in order to 'make it' they eventually lose touch with the innate value of the person hiding behind it. They become a stranger to themselves and a hostage to the very image they worked so hard to create.

WEARING A MASK CAN FEEL SAFE. BUT WORN TOO LONG IT CAN MAKE US A STRANGER TO OURSELVES.

The truth is, we live in a world that's constantly pressuring us to measure up or conform to some idealised image of who we think we're supposed to be. Social expectations, peer pressures, chic branded images, designer-sculpted bodies and photoshopped profile pictures bombard us at every turn. It explains the meteoric rise and rise of cosmetic procedures, the vast majority of which are to tweak and snip and adjust us to look more like what our society has decided is beautiful. The right nose, the right boobs, the right eyes, the right hair, the right abs ... even the right calf muscles! (What, you didn't know your calf muscles aren't defined enough? Oh dear!) It's why so many in Hollywood look just like so many others in Hollywood — and too few look like themselves.

Don't get me wrong, it's only natural to want to feel good about how you look. Certainly vanity is wired in me as strongly as in anyone. I'd be happy to wake up with Jennifer Aniston's body, Angelina Jolie's cheekbones and Pink's abs. But in our society, where cosmetic augmentation is a multibillion-dollar business, refusing to succumb to pressure to act, look and live the way social convention says you should is simultaneously one of the most difficult, courageous and important things you can ever do.

WHEN YOU TRY TO PROVE YOURSELF, YOU DIMINISH YOURSELF.

Like so many people, resisting the pressure to conform is a challenge that's confronted me most of my life. When I moved to Melbourne at 18 to study business at university I quickly became aware of my unsophisticated country ways. I spoke differently (my plural for 'you' was 'yous'), wore my hair differently (frizzy perm, bleached tips), dressed differently ('bogan', as Australians say) and I lacked the social polish of the students I found myself sitting beside in lectures, most of whom had attended elite private schools. Long gone were the days of happily standing out in my class of one at the small (very small!) rural primary school I'd attended. I was now desperate to fit in. Within a year my 'yous' had become 'you' and my homebrand jeans with the triple built-in buckled belts disappeared. I tried hard to dress the *right* way, speak the *right* way, laugh the *right* way and air-kiss the *right* way.

OTHER PEOPLE WON'T VALUE HOW SPECIAL YOU ARE UNLESS YOU DO. OWN YOUR INDIVIDUALITY!

Of course, learning how to present myself well was an adaptive behaviour that ultimately enabled me to succeed professionally. However, many times I remember pretending to be someone I wasn't: more cultured, less country; more refined, less rough around the edges. I often felt as though I was wearing a mask, just waiting to be exposed as an imposter. It was only when I graduated and ventured overseas, where I felt no social pressure, that I realised just how much pressure I'd been putting on myself to fit in. It helped me to see that it's those attributes that make us unique which are ultimately our greatest gifts. So if you want others to value you for who you are, you must first value yourself for who you are.

WHEN ALL YOU DO IS CONFORM, ALL YOU OFFER IS CONFORMITY.

Having the courage to own what makes you different — whether it's your curly hair, your heritage, your sexuality or your penchant for colourful clothes — doesn't set you up for a life of social ostracism or professional banishment. It does the opposite. Because in our superficial, glamorised and often pretentious culture, there's a growing hunger for people who are 'real'; that is, at home with who they are and unwilling to mould themselves otherwise. In short, having the guts to be yourself makes you more attractive to people, not less so. As Coco Chanel once said, 'In order to be irreplaceable, one must always be different'. Indeed, the most successful people — in business and the bigger game of life — are not the ones with the most polished masks; they're the people who refuse to wear one.

DULL YOUR SHINE FOR NO-ONE.

The motto of my high school, Nagle College, was Luceat Lux Vestra: Let your light shine. Letting your light shine is about honouring your talents and dreams and daring to be the fullest expression of who you were created to be. It's about refusing — day in, day out — to dumb or dull yourself down for fear of how others may react. Finally, it's about living authentically, not so you can be better than anybody else, but so you can be the best and brightest version of yourself. And if that sometimes makes others uncomfortable, then so be it. You don't serve anyone when you give into pressures to conform to someone else's view of the world or shrink who you are to ward off the insecurity of others.

YOU HAVE NOTHING TO PROVE TO ANYONE. N.O.T.H.I.N.G!

Being imperfect, as I am, sometimes my insecure ego still gets the better of me and I feel pressured to prove myself in some way or live up to an idealised image. Occasionally it's in a social setting. Other times it's just before I'm about to speak in a public arena, whether on stage or television. But I've gradually become better at noticing when I feel the pressure mounting, and quicker at taking a few deep breaths and asking, 'Who would I be right now if I didn't need to prove anything to anyone?' My answer is never anything such as funny, or clever, or likeable, or insightful, or charismatic. It's always simply 'myself' and it both lightens and liberates me, enabling me to speak more authentically and connect more meaningfully with whoever I'm with — whether it's one person or many. Needless to say, this exercise is always profoundly transformative and I can't recommend it to you highly enough.

WHEN YOU EMBRACE WHO YOU TRULY ARE, YOU ENABLE OTHERS TO DO THE SAME.

Only when we stop trying to prove our worthiness or cover up the aspects of ourselves we fear make us seem unworthy—embracing our personality, however quirky; our heritage, however humble; and our uniqueness, however seemingly imperfect—can we experience true freedom and grow into the fullest, and most authentic, version of ourselves. Conversely, whenever we try to be more than, or less than, or different from who we are, we unconsciously relinquish our freedom, rendering ourselves a prisoner to the social norms and expectations of those we aspire to impress.

Years ago I decided to embrace the saying, 'You can take the girl out of the country, but you can't take the country out of the girl'. It was my way of owning the sometimes 'rough-around-the-edges' rural roots that shaped me into who I am. Likewise, you also weren't born to be like everybody else. You were born to shine brightly and live truthfully ... however odd you are! So never let your fear of standing apart from the crowd keep you from owning all that makes you, *you*. Because, as Carly shows people so powerfully every time she walks out of her home and into a judgemental world, when you embrace what makes you different, you implicitly give others permission to do the same. Everyone is better off. Try it.

Train the brave

Brené Brown wrote that 'authenticity is the daily practice of letting go who you think you're supposed to be and embracing who you are'. So how would you act, speak and express yourself differently if you were to let go who you think you're 'supposed to be' and honour all that makes you different, even if it means standing out? How is it costing you not to?

CHAPTER 9
Change before you have to

The Sahara Desert, which spreads across 9.4 million square kilometres, is larger than Australia and almost as large as the United States. Most years it grows by about 50 kilometres, but during a decade-long drought in the 1980s it grew much faster. I decided to cross it, soon after, in late 1991. Arriving from Morocco on a truck with a group of other intrepid travellers, I crossed into Algeria and then went south across the vast swathes of scorched desert into Niger and on to Nigeria.

Despite having grown up in Australia, one of the most desert-laden countries in the world, up until then I'd never spent any time in a desert. The arid landscape, with its infertile sand dunes stretching nearly 200 metres high and spreading out over thousands of kilometres, was striking. With scorching days and freezing nights, I was in awe of the resilience its nomad dwellers showed against the fierce Harmattan winds, which sandblasted their way across the Sahara at that time of year.

One image still etched in my memory was of an elderly man sitting on an old drum of some sort beside the remnants of a building, which I assumed must have once been his home. Dressed in the voluminous robes and indigo dyed turban of the Taureg people, who have inhabited this region for thousands of years, what struck me about him was that the dwelling he sat in front of had been consumed by the burnt desert sands some time before. Around him was nothing inhabitable for it had all been consumed by the thousands of tonnes of sand blown by the desert winds. There was no vegetation, nothing besides a weary date tree. No respite from the unforgiving sun apart from the small shadows cast by the walls of the building, which were still awaiting burial.

But there he sat. I wondered how long he'd been sitting there and how long he'd continue to do so before he accepted that the life he once lived had been buried by the sands that marked his existence.

I never did find out. After passing by, our truck soon moved on southwards across the wide sea of desert plains into the sub-Sahel and central Africa.

BECAUSE LIFE IS THE WAY IT IS, IT CAN NEVER STAY THE WAY IT IS.

Thinking of that man reminds me of summer days in my childhood spent building sandcastles on Ninety Mile Beach in the East Gippsland region of Victoria, Australia. My brothers and sisters and I would spend hours building elaborate towers and moat systems only to have the tide slowly creep in and, wave by wave, pull our magnificent creation back into the sea. We'd do our best to rebuild our masterpiece, but alas, there was nothing we could do to stem the tide and eventually we would concede defeat.

CHANGE IS INEVITABLE. IT'S OUR ATTACHMENT TO PERMANENCE THAT CREATES OUR SUFFERING.

Whether it's the desert sands, the ocean tides, the changing weather or the passing of time, the sooner we surrender to what we can't change, the sooner we can produce something new and the less angst, pain and heartache we'll create for ourselves along the way. The reality is that denying change prolongs our pain and deprives us of the opportunities that change always holds, albeit they're sometimes hidden opportunities. Rather than build the new, we consume ourselves with preserving the old. Ultimately, it's the illusion of permanence, our attachment to things remaining the same, that makes change so much more difficult than it needs to be.

Look around you now. What is it that's changing that you wish weren't? Where are you fighting against forces over which you have no control? Where have you been trying to create an outcome that will never be because you've been unwilling to accept larger forces at play that prevent it?

WHEN YOU STOP CLINGING TO THE PAST IT RELEASES YOU TO IMPROVE YOUR FUTURE.

Refusing to acknowledge the forces of change can eventually land you in a tough spot, with few options, a lot of needless self-induced pain and much forced learning in order to adapt to the reality you've been denying. Just ask the guy who used to head up Kodak.

While it takes courage to dare to change the world around us, it also takes courage to accept what can't be changed. It's not about giving up on the future. It's about letting go of a past state that can no longer be part of it. In letting go of the attachment you've had to what can no longer be, you open your heart, mind and future to a new horizon of possibilities and expand your capacity to create something different from before and, very likely, something even better.

Train the brave

Focus your energy not on trying to change what can't be altered, but on changing what can. Where have you been channelling your energy into something to no avail? What is it that you need to accept as unchangeable? By making peace with forces beyond your control, what new opportunities might open up that may have otherwise escaped your attention? How can you seize them?

CHAPTER 10
Live by design, not by default

Two months prior to meeting my husband Andrew I'd returned from a year of backpacking around the world. So on our first date I think he hardly got a word in as I regaled him with my adventures. (He'd probably tell you nothing's changed, which would be nonsense!) We were engaged the following year (another time where my intuition served me well) and married 10 months later. During that 'honeymoon' period we talked a lot about the life we wanted to create together. We wanted at least three kids, maybe four. We wanted to share adventures and we wanted to spend time working and living abroad.

At the time, we both worked for large multinationals so we set about speaking with our employers about the possibility of international assignments. I was thinking London, New York, Hong Kong ... somewhere cosmopolitan and pulsing with life. So, I remember the evening when Andrew and I sat down to a pasta dinner and he shared a promising conversation he'd had that day with his manager about a possible overseas posting. I also remember nearly choking on my meatball when he said where: Papua New Guinea. While it wasn't our ideal destination, it was the only offer on the table, so we decided, 'What the heck!'

Four months later we were packing our belongings into boxes to embark on a three-year assignment living in PNG's capital Port Moresby, an adventure that would both shape us and expand the horizon of our life together. Of course, not everyone is excited by the idea of living abroad, particularly not in a city rated as one of the world's least liveable (outranked only by Dhaka). However, unless you take time to decide what you want to paint upon the canvas of your life, how will you know where to focus your time, which opportunities to pursue and seize, which to decline and the sorts of people you want to share your journey with? You won't.

BRAVERY ALONE IS NOT ENOUGH. IT MUST BE CHANNELLED TOWARD A BIGGER VISION.

Too many people spend more time thinking about what they want to do on their annual holiday than what they want to do with their life. With no clear intention about the life they want to create, they can end up meandering through their days, living aimlessly and passively at the mercy of the circumstances that happen upon them. Any area of your life where you have no vision of what you intend to create lacks a personal compass to help you navigate forward. Without that compass it's all too easy to find yourself living like a ship adrift at sea, at the whim of the winds, tides and currents and you are likely to end up in a place you would never consciously have chosen. As former UN Secretary General Kofi Annan wrote, 'To live is to choose, but to choose well, you must know who you are and what you stand for, where you want to go and why you want to get there'.

I'm not saying that you have to know exactly what you want to be doing or where you want to be living 10 years from now, nor the specific person you'll marry or what you'll call your children or where'll you retire. I'm simply saying that if you aren't clear about the types of pursuits, experiences and relationships that 'fill your cup', you can end up with either an empty one or a full one that leaves you indifferent, despairing or hungry for something else.

Living by design is about being intentional about what you do each day, clear about why you do what you do and why you don't do what you don't do. It's about being willing to take a step back, polishing the lens through which you're viewing the world, challenging your perceptions, cross-examining your choices and reassessing your actions. It's about letting go the fear that you're supposed to be anywhere else than where you are right now, but having the courage to be more deliberate about what you want for your future.

YOU CAN'T LIVE INTENTIONALLY IF YOU'RE FOREVER LIVING HURRIEDLY.

So how do you do that? You start by giving yourself permission to slow down. To stop running. Stop hurrying. Stop multitasking. Stop turning yourself inside out in an effort to be all things to all people. Only when you stop with all your busy 'doing' can you reconnect to your 'being' and to what you yearn for most. Then, and only then, will you be able to muster up the courage to say 'no' to whatever you've been doing that doesn't move you towards it and shout a big, brave '*YES!*' to what does.

Whatever the state of your heart, your health or your life right now, there's nothing — *nothing* — stopping you from starting right now to live your life by design, rather than by default. There's nothing — *nothing* — stopping you from taking five minutes right now to make peace with your past and to connect with your heart's deepest longing for your future. And there's nothing — *nothing* — stopping you right now from breathing deeply, really deeply, right to the bottom of your soul, so that you can get fully present to the wonder that is your life. To accepting it, cherishing it, marvelling at it for all that it is, and for all that it isn't, so that you can re-engage with the world more purposefully, more compassionately and more wholeheartedly.

CLARIFYING YOUR HIGHEST INTENTION FOR YOUR LIFE WILL TRANSFORM HOW YOU LIVE IT.

Creating a vision for your life and then working intentionally towards it won't insulate you from life's unexpected trials, twists and turns. (I had three miscarriages and a gun pointed at my head in an armed robbery during my time in Papua New Guinea.) But it will put you in the driver's seat, helping you to see where you need to speak up, push back, step out or forge a different path from the one others want for you. And when your world tilts on its axis (as it inevitably will), living your life intentionally — by design, not default — will help you get back on your feet faster. It will also help you notice beauty you may otherwise have missed and deepen your gratitude for all the experiences that have brought you to where you are right now and have shaped the person you've become. Whether or not you're conscious of it, every intention sets energy into motion ... for better or worse. Set your highest intention for your life and you can't go wrong.

Train the brave

Everything good in the world once began with a positive intention. So begin something good in your life today by giving yourself a few minutes to clarify your highest intention in each of the following areas of your life (feel free to add to or modify these to work for you):

» *Family and home life.* What are your highest intentions for your closest relationships? What sort of environment do you want to create at home? How do you want to feel about those you live with and love most? How do you want them to treat and feel about you?

» *Other relationships.* What kinds of relationships do you want to invest in, personally and professionally? What would there be more of? What would there be less of?

» *Health and wellbeing.* What is your highest intention for your optimal wellbeing — body, mind and spirit?

» *Wealth and finances.* What relationship do you want to have with money? What do you need to attend to in order to create the sense of prosperity you seek?

» *Work, career and business.* What is your highest intention for the work you do each day and the impact it makes on others? What strengths do you want to nurture? Who are you when you are at your best at work?

» *Recreation and hobbies.* What activities would bring you a greater sense of fulfilment, joy and fun? What will make you feel more whole, healthy and fully alive?

» *Community and contribution.* What contribution do you want to make? What importance do you want to place on kindness, generosity and compassion?

Part II
Speak bravely

How to have courageous conversations about things that matter

CHAPTER 11

Your voice matters; be heard

When Malala Yousafzai was 15 years old she was shot in the face by members of the Taliban while riding home on the school bus. They were unhappy that she publicly advocated for the right of girls to be educated and were unwilling to tolerate it any longer. While the Taliban had hoped to silence Malala, their cowardly violence only steeled her resolve. After her recovery she said, 'The only thing that happened when I got shot was that weakness, fear and hopelessness died. Strength, power and courage were born'.

While Malala, now a Nobel Laureate, had been outspoken in her belief that all girls should have access to quality education before, she was now even more determined that speaking up for the rights of women was a cause worth committing to, even if it put her life at risk. Malala's courage to put her life on the line to speak against a regime and culture that oppresses women is fuelled by her knowledge that the cause she's fighting for, and the future she's committed to, demand no less. As Malala has said, 'I raise up my voice — not so that I can shout, but so that those without a voice can be heard'.

It's hard not to be inspired by Malala's courage. But the truth is that every one of us has things to say that need to be heard; and we all, like Malala, have the ability to speak more bravely. But to do so we must first take responsibility for ensuring that we're heard and not sit around waiting to be asked. It could be a long wait!

DON'T LET TIMIDITY KEEP YOU FROM SAYING WHAT NEEDS TO BE HEARD.

Having your voice heard in a noisy, self-interested world demands courage — courage to believe in the value of what you have to say, and courage to rise above the age-old instinct to seek pleasure and to avoid pain (which includes being shot!). Indeed, every action we take is motivated by these two drivers, and speaking bravely is no less.

Our motivations for doing anything are influenced by a complex web of unconscious drivers and cognitive biases that impair our ability to accurately predict what will bring us the greatest pleasure or the least pain over the long haul. It's why smart people sometimes do daft things. And it's why you can probably quickly recall numerous times you wish you'd spoken up more honestly, more bravely or more assertively, but you didn't. Fear won out.

When it comes to speaking bravely — to sticking your neck out and taking a risk — you're wired to focus more on the immediate costs of speaking up than you are on the long-term costs of silence. Just think about saying something really courageous today and very quickly your focus will move to the immediate consequences you'll have to face if it doesn't go well. And while you may also be able to imagine how you'll feel a year from now if you say nothing, the prospect of experiencing the immediate cost (whether it's embarrassment, rejection, confrontation, disappointment or conflict) tends to win out.

FOR THE SAKE OF WHAT ARE YOU WILLING TO SPEAK UP? DON'T DISCOUNT THE COST OF SILENCE.

Over the course of your life, there will be countless times you'll be called on to speak bravely: asking for what you want, saying no to what you don't, giving candid feedback, admitting you're wrong and sharing your vulnerability. While no two conversations are ever the same, every single one of them demands you to expose yourself to a reaction that may be difficult to handle and to emotions that are uncomfortable to feel. Our innate aversion to discomfort explains why so many people — when considering whether to speak up, step up, make a change or take a chance — lean away from the inherent risk rather than towards it. It's why so many relationships fall apart — not because of the differences that arise, but because they were left to fester. It's also why you have to be super clear — and I mean *uber crystalline clear* — in your answer to this question:

For the sake of what are you willing to speak up?

That is, for the sake of what are you willing to make yourself vulnerable and risk the pain of losing something you value: your pride, your reputation, your money, your time, your job, social approval or professional admiration? Every act of courage is about laying something you value on the line for something you value even more. Speaking bravely takes no less. Until you're clear about what you value more than what you get from sticking with the status quo — comfort, safety, predictability, familiarity, approval — you'll be without any compelling reason to put it at risk.

COURAGEOUS CONVERSATIONS BEGIN WITH YOUR DECISION THAT SPEAKING THE TRUTH IS MORE IMPORTANT THAN AVOIDING RISK.

'To thine own self be true,' said William Shakespeare. Selling out on what's true for us may not inflict a great pain on you today, or tomorrow. But over time, when you forsake your own truth, staying silent when your voice needs to be heard, you run the greater risk of — to paraphrase Thoreau — living a life of quiet desperation and going to the grave with the song still in you.

For the sake of what are you willing to speak bravely?

For the sake of your integrity?

For the sake of your dreams?

For the sake of your family?

For the sake of your organisation's big mission?

For the sake of your health?

For the sake of the oppressed?

For the sake of a better future?

For the sake of those who love you?

For the sake of not being a doormat for others to walk on?

For the sake of those whose sacrifice you want to honour?

For the sake of never having to wonder, 'What if?'

You decide.

Malala Yousafzai wrote in her book *I Am Malala,* 'If people were silent nothing would change'. Likewise, every courageous conversation begins by making the decision that giving voice to your truth is more important than the risk of what might happen when you do. Just know that your voice matters. Your opinions count. Your words influence. Never doubt it — or yourself. But rather, speak bravely for the sake of something more important than your pride or the possibility of hurting someone else's. What you yearn for most is riding on it.

Train the brave

The Roman historian Tacitus wrote, 'The desire for safety stands against every great and noble enterprise'. The desire to be emotionally safe is also what stands against us, ensuring that our voices are heard. For the sake of what are you willing to speak your truth, even if your voice shakes?

CHAPTER 12

Speak from your heart, not your ego

Your conversations are powerful. They hold the power to grow influence and trust, or to weaken it. They can open doors of opportunity and possibility or quickly close them. Conversations can trigger family feuds that last for decades. They can also heal old wounds and pave new pathways to peace: in our homes, communities and throughout the world. Indeed, the words you speak can make a profound and lasting impact on those around you — for better or worse.

A few years back I had the opportunity of working with a colonel in the United States military. He'd done multiple tours of duty in Iraq and Afghanistan, leading numerous missions that had required putting his life on the line. It's fair to say he fit the bill when it came to being courageous. After completing his tours of duty he was assigned to a senior administrative post at the Pentagon. It was there that he found himself needing to build a whole new type of courage: 'conversational courage'. Though he'd excelled at executing the orders of his superiors, he struggled when speaking up to challenge them and when giving candid feedback — two skills essential to excelling in his new role.

BEING BRAVE IN YOUR CONVERSATIONS CAN BE JUST AS SCARY AS BEING BRAVE ON THE BATTLEFIELD.

His situation highlights the reality of courage: that being brave extends far beyond heroic actions on the battlefield. In fact, most of the time being brave is far less dramatic, far more mundane and easier to avoid without appearing cowardly. It requires us not to confront an external enemy, but to confront the enemy within ourselves — our fear, our ego and our insecurity — which drives us to fit in and to preserve the image we want others to see. Nowhere is this more relevant than in how we connect and communicate with those around us. Not just about the really big issues, but about the everyday small ones that can slowly compound, fester away and ultimately derail our relationships, careers and lives.

THE MOST IMPORTANT CONVERSATIONS ARE OFTEN THE MOST DIFFICULT.

Harnessing the power of conversation in your work, your relationships and your life all boils down to your willingness to park your pride and step outside your conversational comfort zone. As simple as it sounds, many people struggle to say what they think, to share how they feel, to reveal where they face difficulty and to ask for what they need. Which is why speaking truthfully is one of the most courageous things you can ever do. It's also one of the most important because the health of your relationships, your career and your heart depend on it.

It takes courage to step out of your conversational comfort zone — to speak up and give voice to the things that truly matter to you. It takes courage to make a stand for yourself or for those who can't speak for themselves. And it takes courage to say things that will make you vulnerable to judgement, rejection or disappointing people you care for. It's why so many people choose to stay silent: their fear of speaking up about what weighs them down exceeds their commitment to changing it.

Too often we choose the certainty of an issue remaining unaddressed because we're afraid of the possibility of an awkward conversation. Perhaps you've walked that path yourself—choosing to step around an issue or pretend everything is fine when in fact you're feeling upset, alone, hurt, frustrated, resentful or outright angry. If so, you aren't alone.

'Oh, I could never do that,' Vanessa said to me when I suggested that she speak to her boss about how she felt she was constantly being passed over for promotional opportunities.

'We don't have those kinds of conversations,' Debbie confided after I suggested she speak to her husband about how isolated she felt in her marriage.

While addressing sensitive issues—where emotions can run high and sensitivities deep—may never be easy, the price you pay for avoiding an uncomfortable conversation far exceeds the discomfort you feel in having it.

WHAT ISN'T TALKED OUT GETS ACTED OUT.

Issues that aren't put on the table for open discussion and debate, but left to fester, always find a way of expressing themselves. It's rarely constructive. More often, issues that aren't talked out end up being acted out as snide remarks, subtle innuendos, passive aggression, manipulation or the 'silent treatment'. 'No big deal', we tell ourselves, 'everyone does it'. But over time, the lack of oxygen turns petty grumbles into major grievances.

People walk out of their jobs or their marriages. Or, short of physically leaving, they emotionally and mentally check out. It exacts a steep toll on their performance and relationships, as well as their happiness and health. Medical research has shown a higher incidence of heart disease and other serious conditions in people who have felt resentment for extended periods of time.

Seven keys to a courageous conversation

Never underestimate the impact of a courageous conversation. When you decide to put issues on the table (however uncomfortable that may feel)—to share how you feel with dignity, respect and a genuine intention to improve a situation—you'll find that you not only build more trusting and rewarding relationships, but that you grow your influence and, with it, your confidence to address other issues that arise in the future.

1. Start with heart

What comes from the heart lands on the heart. So begin by clarifying your highest intention for the other person, for yourself and for those your relationship impacts. When you enter a conversation—not to prove you're right or to make someone else wrong, but to create a better outcome for all—your words land differently from when your pride, anger or ego are running the show.

2. Find the common ground

While you may want something different from someone else, if you keep zooming up, there will be things that you both want and concerns you both share. Speak from that place: from a mutual goal or concern you both want and care about. For example, 'I know we both care about making this [project, marriage, team] work and want to feel [valued, supported, respected] in it'.

3. Express your opinion as just that

When you express your opinion as though it's the one and only truth, you're guaranteed to get others offside. Rather, express your perspective as just that—*your* perspective—and then share how it makes you feel using 'I' statements. Feelings are never wrong or right; they just are. Doing so removes the judgement so the other person doesn't feel you're making them wrong or belittling their opinion (which is always counterproductive). For example, 'I feel undervalued and embarrassed when I'm cut off midsentence in front of others' will be heard and responded to differently from saying, 'You don't value me and always embarrass me'. One shares; the other accuses.

4. Distinguish the person from their behaviour

If you're unhappy about what someone has done or failed to do, be careful to disentangle *who* they are from *what* they've done. Someone may have acted thoughtlessly, but by labelling them as thoughtless, careless or cavalier you imply they can't be any other way. Instead of boxing people in, use language in ways that leave open the possibility for positive change.

5. Act big when others act small

Emotions are highly contagious, so when someone is acting small-minded or petulant, mean or just outright rude, resist the temptation to respond in kind. Hold the high ground and stay calm, even if they're getting

(continued)

Seven keys to a courageous conversation *(cont'd)*

upset or throwing accusations. No matter who it is, what they did or how strongly you hold them in the wrong (because, damn it, they are!), always act with the character, courage and calmness they may be lacking. It's rarely easy to swallow, but it's those people who annoy and upset you the most who have the most to teach you.

6. Be careful what your body is saying

Your way of being communicates far more loudly than your words. So be mindful of how you're holding yourself, your tone of voice and facial expressions. You may not be aware of these, but the person you're speaking to is.

7. Focus forward

It's easy to get pulled into 'who shoulda-woulda-coulda' conversations, stone throwing and name-calling. But to what end? Keep your conversations future focused. How would you like things to be in the future? What needs to start happening? What needs to stop? Be as specific as you can. In the interim, you may simply have to agree to stay in dialogue and navigate the best path forward.

You succeed or fail one conversation at a time. My colonel friend's experience showed that engaging in conversations that require us to lay our vulnerability on the line can sometimes feel every bit as dangerous as laying our life on the line. Even when, intellectually, we know it's not! Which is why you need to trust in yourself that if there's something you genuinely want to say, chances are there's someone who genuinely needs to hear it. Your conversations have the power not just to change lives, but to change history — starting with your own.

DON'T WAIT TO OOZE CONFIDENCE BEFORE YOU SHARE WHAT'S WEIGHING YOU DOWN.

Poet Thomas Fuller wrote, 'All things are difficult before they are easy'. And so it is with talking about issues that make you feel intensely uncomfortable. While I don't know what conversations you need to have right now, I do know that you have the ability to speak up about any issue with any person at any time. You may not have mustered up the courage until now or mastered the skill, but you have within you the ability to do both. You just need practice. So don't wait until you have the self-confidence of Bill Clinton or the eloquence of Oprah before you step courageously into conversations about the things that matter most. Take a deep breath, then open your mouth and share your truth. In the end, it's no more or less difficult than that.

Train the brave

What's going on in your life that's calling for you to engage in a courageous conversation? What's the cost of not addressing it? If you were going to be really brave today, what would you share? What would you reveal? What would you challenge? What would you ask for? Get clear about your highest intentions for yourself and others; take a deep breath, then speak from your heart. It will make all the difference.

CHAPTER 13

Say no to the good to say yes to the great

If you're like me (and a few million other people who like to please others), you've probably kicked yourself numerous times after saying yes to something you didn't really want to do. Or maybe you genuinely did want to do it, but you already had too much on your plate to take on one more thing. The word 'no' may be just one tiny, little, monosyllabic, two-letter word, yet it's one so many people have such a hard time saying. 'Yes' is so much easier!

The term 'people pleaser' was coined to describe the pressure and pull many of us feel to say yes and make commitments that push other priorities and values down the list. The truth is that saying no is harder than saying yes. People want you to say yes and so when you do, you get an immediate hit of people-pleasing gratification. Saying no, on the other hand, puts you at risk of causing disappointment, hurting feelings or falling out with the pack. It's why yes rolls quickly off the tongue before our brains have kicked fully into gear.

Of course, saying yes to life's diverse array of opportunities and adventures can also be an act of courage. But having the capacity to do so requires knowing when we need to say no instead. Sometimes, in our efforts to be all things to all people, we wind up stressed out, burnt out, breaking promises and too exhausted to say yes to the things we care about most. We're simply too over-committed and overwhelmed to contemplate them!

In my own life, learning how to say no has been an ongoing journey: two steps forward, one step back. Sometimes I still mess up and commit to things for the wrong reasons, or end up overcommitted and spread too thin. But by taking time to get clear about what I want to give a big 'yes!' to, I've slowly (oh-so-slowly) become better at it. For instance, making the time to write this book, in between being mum (cook, taxi driver, counsellor and administrative manager) to my four kids, speaking engagements, coaching clients, media segments and other writing deadlines, I've had to say no more times and to more people than I'd have liked. Hopefully, as you read this now, you're glad that I did (because it wasn't easy!).

A 'ONCE-IN-A-LIFETIME' OPPORTUNITY IS IRRELEVANT IF IT'S NOT ALIGNED WITH WHAT YOU MOST WANT AND VALUE.

Numerous times people have shared with me that they said yes to something because it was a 'once-in-a-lifetime' opportunity, then later regretted it. Whether you'll ever get the same opportunity again is irrelevant if it's not moving you in a direction you want to go!

Unless you're clear about what you most want to say a big 'yes!' to in both the short and long term, you won't have the clarity and courage required to say no to those things that aren't aligned with your most important values, aspirations and goals. So before you fill up your calendar, decide what you most want to fill it up with, then schedule those things in lest everything else landing on your plate each day crowds them out.

IF YOU'RE SAYING YES SIMPLY BECAUSE YOU THINK YOU 'SHOULD', THEN PERHAPS YOU SHOULDN'T.

There are lots of fun, worthwhile and never-again-to-be-repeated things you can say yes to. There always will be. And, of course, sometimes you have to jump at opportunities and commit to things even though they create a conflict with other priorities (every working parent's lot). I've found that when what you naturally commit to aligns with what you're most committed to, balance sorts itself out.

Likewise, throughout your life, your values and priorities will change. What's most important is that you're clear in your own mind about why you're spending time on the things you are and why you aren't spending time on the things you aren't! If you're doing it simply because you feel that you 'should', then you probably shouldn't. Our 'shoulds' tend to be driven by social expectations and pressures, rather than by our own deepest wants. By replacing the word 'should' with 'could' and then adding in an alternative option, it removes the judgement. For instance, 'I should go to this dinner' becomes 'I could go to this dinner or I could spend the evening with my family'. Even so, saying no can be hard, so here are a few suggestions on how you can.

How to say no with more grace and less guilt

Even when you're clear about why you need to say no, you may still baulk at the prospect of letting people down or causing offence. People have asked you to do something for a reason—they want you to say 'yes'! Here are three ways to help you say no with more grace and less guilt.

1. Separate the person from their request

Our reticence to say no tends to come from our desire to spare someone's feelings: to make them feel valued. So ensure they know you're saying no to what they're asking, not *to* them. You can use the word 'however' to distinguish between the two. For example, 'Sam, I'd love to join you for lunch; however, I have a lot on at the moment and I really can't find the time this week. How about a coffee later this month?'

2. Negotiate what you're committing to

Every commitment involves a *what* and a *when*. So you can always make a counter offer and say yes to one aspect of what's being asked of you, but not to the whole thing, or not on the same timeline. For example, 'Chris, I'd love to join your committee, but I'm not in a position to chair it. Can I help with the publicity?'

3. Offer to get back to them later

An excellent tactic for hardcore people pleasers is getting into a habit of offering to get back to someone later (specify exactly when). Doing so buys you time to decide whether you're up to it, and if not, to prepare a confident and gracious no. Just be careful you don't add to your pressure by saying 'maybe' when you want to say 'no'.

BEFORE YOU SAY YES TO OTHERS, BE SURE YOU AREN'T SAYING NO TO YOURSELF.

Of course, having the courage to say no isn't always just about the everyday requests, invitations and opportunities that present themselves. Sometimes we have to say no to the current trajectory of our lives, to the people we're spending time with or the career path we've taken. I shared a story in my first book, *Find Your Courage,* about my sister Anne's decision to break off an engagement six weeks out from her wedding. It wasn't that her fiancé wasn't a 'good guy'. He was a terrific guy. It was that she just didn't feel inspired about spending her life with him. As I said to her at the time — while she wrestled with finding the courage to end the relationship and the hurt she knew she would cause — getting married to someone because you're afraid they're the best you can do, you're worried about hurting their feelings or simply because you're scared of the fallout is never a good reason to do it. It's not a good reason to do most things! Saying no is an act of respect; respect for yourself, and respect for others.

DON'T 'SHOULD' ON YOURSELF OR LET OTHERS 'SHOULD' ON YOU.

Most of us live in an environment that's constantly pulling, pressuring, guilting and shoulding us into saying yes to things that aren't aligned with what we want most. So every day you must be intentional about reconnecting with what that is, digging deep and then saying no to all that doesn't serve your greatest good in this world (and anything that doesn't serve your greatest good, by default, doesn't serve anyone else's ... although not everyone will see it that way!). Over the years, I've really admired people who have done that — even when it's me they're saying no to! It's taught me that when you say no to others — kindly and for the reasons that serve the highest good—you not only empower them in doing so themselves, but you earn their respect and nurture your own.

In the end there's often no escaping the moment when you know you're letting someone down or causing disappointment. Which is why saying no requires you to find the courage to step into that place of discomfort, clear that something more important lies at stake, and honouring your highest priorities, your deepest aspirations and what matters the very most to you. To quote Piet Hein, 'He who lets the small things bind him, leaves the great undone behind him'. Whether it's spending time on caring for yourself or someone you hold dear, or pursuing that dream you've too long ignored, leave nothing great undone behind you for fear of of what might happen if you say no.

Train the brave

What do you need to say no to today that will allow you to focus on more important priorities? What do you need to say no to in the bigger scheme of your life in order to create space for something that aligns with your deepest values, passions and dreams?

CHAPTER 14
Dare to ask big

Think of a situation that's causing you to feel some emotional angst or frustration, overwhelm, resentment or even desperation! Go on, surely there's at least one!

If you aren't getting something you want, or you are tolerating something you don't want, it's generally a sign that there's an unmade request. Maybe it's a boss who has unreasonable expectations. Perhaps it's a colleague who doesn't seem to pull their weight. Perhaps it's your partner who's doing something that upsets you. Or maybe there's someone you haven't even met who has the power, or purse strings, to give you something you really want, but they have no idea that you want it!

Needless to say, complaining about your problems doesn't solve them, and whining about unmet needs doesn't fulfil them. If there's something you really want, you have to be willing to ask for it.

PEOPLE AREN'T MIND READERS, SO DON'T ASSUME PEOPLE KNOW WHAT YOU WANT.

You get what you tolerate and you teach people how to treat you. If you passively allow others to take you for granted, to overstep boundaries or to treat you unfairly, then you are complicit in it. Taking responsibility for letting others know what you want (and don't want) is fundamental to your success. Indeed, it's a rule of life that it will only pay as much as you're willing to ask for.

Too often, though, we assume the people around us — our boss, colleagues and even our spouse and friends — know what we want and need. But people aren't mind readers and assuming they know what's on your mind can be a sure-fire recipe for resentment. For any relationship to thrive, both parties have to take responsibility for communicating their needs. Hints just don't cut it. If you'd like your boss to consider you for a promotion, you need to let them know that. If you'd like a colleague to change how they're dealing with a situation, you also need to convey that to them. Expecting people to read your mind isn't only unrealistic, it's unfair on them.

FEAR OF NOT GETTING WHAT YOU WANT IS A POOR REASON NOT TO ASK FOR IT.

Let's face it, often the reason we often don't ask for what we want is because we're afraid we won't get it or that we're not worthy of it. When I interviewed Lisa Messenger — founder of *Renegade Collective* magazine — for Raw Courage TV, she shared with me how she had set up hundreds of meetings with companies to help her get her magazine off the ground. After many attempts at landing a meeting with the marketing manager from one of Australia's biggest banks, she finally got his interest by sending him a tweet asking for a meeting. 'How about 2 pm tomorrow?' he tweeted back. It was on!

Ahead of the meeting, Lisa was nervous. This man's decision could launch her dream or send it spiralling. 'I almost didn't want to have the meeting because it meant I would have my answer,' she shared with me. 'A definitive no would be a massive blow.' But she wasn't backing out. She put on her best outfit and when he asked how much she needed, she asked big. 'We'll do it!' he said. In that moment *Renegade Collective* was officially born. Now sold in more than 30 countries (and counting!), it all came from a big dream and a bold request.

ASKING FOR WHAT YOU WANT CORRELATES VERY HIGHLY WITH GETTING IT.

Not only can fear keep us from asking for *what* we want, it can keep us from asking for *all* we want. We're afraid of appearing too pushy or too demanding, or of putting people on the spot. But to create the possibility of getting what you truly want, you have to have the courage to risk all of the above. You have to lay your vulnerability on the line and risk the rejection, risk the awkwardness or risk whatever's kept you suffering until now. It's a general rule of life that you'll rarely, if ever, be given more than what you have the courage to ask for. Asking for what you want tends to correlate strongly with getting it.

NO IS THE RISK YOU MUST TAKE TO GET YES. TAKE IT. JUST NEVER MAKE A 'NO' MEAN MORE THAN IT DOES.

The reality is that you won't always get what you ask for. Such is life. Don't take it personally. Rather, accept it graciously as a 'no for now', and then move on. At least now you know where you stand and can plan accordingly. More so, by letting people know what you want, and showing you've got the guts to ask for it, other doors of opportunity may open your way. Bravery does that — it attracts opportunity.

So if you want something more or different from what you've been getting, have the courage to ask for it. Don't dilute your requests in order to minimise the possibility of being turned down. Rather, embrace the 'go big or go home' mindset that Lisa Messenger does. Think about what your ideal outcome would be and then confidently, courageously, ask for it.

GIVE PEOPLE THE OPPORTUNITY TO SAY YES. DON'T SAY NO FOR THEM.

While you may not always get as much as you asked for (whether it be a pay rise, funding your start-up or having your kids make their rooms spotlessly clean), you're going to get a lot more than what you would have otherwise. So stand tall, breathe deep and ask big. When you find the courage to ask for what you really want, you may find that you actually get it! Honestly, what have you got to lose?

Train the brave

If you don't ask, the answer will always be no. So think of something you'd like more of: more money, more support, more opportunity, more open communication, more feedback, more respect or more responsibility. Now identify a specific request you can make to address what you want more of, and then make a commitment to ask for it as soon as is practical (ideally within the next day!). Go on ... be bold! You won't regret you did, but you may long regret it if you don't.

CHAPTER 15
Listen to understand; not to be understood

We all like to think we're right. None of us likes to think we're wrong. It's a human thing.

Of course, this wouldn't be a problem if we all saw things exactly the same way, but alas, you only have to look at the wars raging across the world, in our houses of government and in our own homes to see that we don't. So when it comes to getting along with the other seven billion human beings that inhabit planet Earth with us, it's inevitable that beliefs, desires and agendas will collide. Whether we work these out through vigorous debate or by waging full-blown war, it all boils down to the willingness of all parties to respect the right of others to hold their own opinion and to try to understand it. Doing this requires what I believe is the most important of all communication tools: listening.

COMMUNICATION IS NOT DEFINED BY WHAT IS SAID, BUT BY WHAT IS HEARD.

Have you ever told what you thought was a super funny joke that only caused offence? Living in the United States for more than 10 years taught me that the sarcasm Australians use without a second thought can be interpreted as outright insolence by many Americans. That's not because Americans don't have a sense of humour; it's because they have a different style of humour. It's just not as funny as ours! (And yes, that's sarcasm.)

Needless to say, I'm no expert on how to tell jokes so that people will laugh at them. I'm still figuring that out myself—and my kids will gladly tell you that I've got a *loooong* way to go. The point of this chapter is to help you find the courage you need to give up being right about your way of seeing (and doing and saying) things, and become more open to how others see them. Why? Because the meaning of communication is not defined by what's being *said*, it's defined by what's being *heard*. Knowing how others will hear what you're saying ultimately boils down to one thing: your ability to put yourself in their shoes and 'speak to their listening'.

LISTENING ISN'T RELOADING.

Of course, deep-level listening is not always required for communicating well, such as when you're telling someone tomorrow's weather forecast or giving directions (actually, deep-level listening is required when I'm getting directions!). However, when it comes to issues where emotions can run high, becoming fully present to who you're with and listening deeply — to both what's being said, and even more importantly, to what's not being said — can make a profound difference. You can't do this while doing anything else at the same time. When people feel that you're sincerely trying to understand where they're coming from — and not just placating them — not only will they feel more valued, but they'll be much more likely to genuinely try to understand where you're coming from too.

IF YOU WANT TO BE LISTENED TO, YOU SHOULD MAKE TIME TO LISTEN.

Listening with the sincere intention of understanding requires rising above the instinctive desire to jump in and point out where others are mistaken or misguided. That doesn't mean you don't think they've got it wrong; it means you're trying to understand not just what they think, but how they came to think that way. Doing so takes courage because it requires parking your attachment to your 'truth', and opening your mind and heart to the possibility that there are other ways of seeing things that are just as valid as how you see them — perhaps even more so. As I say, it takes courage.

The best listening comes from a place of genuine curiosity. It demands that you not only try to walk in someone else's shoes to *see* as they do, but that you try to *feel* as they do. Allowing yourself to feel their spoken and unspoken fears, their hurt, their resentment and even their heartache can be very uncomfortable. These emotions aren't easy, yet emotions drive behaviour far more than logic alone and so appreciating how someone is feeling can help you to work through your differences far more effectively than relying solely on logic can.

LET THE SILENCE DO ITS WORK.

Most people feel uncomfortable with silence. It's awkward. That's why we jump in to fill it. But the more emotions that are at play, the more important it is to leave the silence to do its work. Because it's in that quiet space where nothing is being said that people are able to sift through their thoughts and process their emotions. Having the courage to allow the silence can lead to the heart of what the conversation *really* needs to be about.

The word 'listen' has the same letters as the word 'silent'. Ironic huh? But too often in our silence we aren't truly listening ... we're just reloading, waiting for our turn to jump back in and fire our next shot. So as you think about the issues weighing down your relationships right now, consider where your failure to truly listen to what others have to say — to consider what they *aren't* willing to say and to understand how they feel — may have only widened the divide and fuelled animosity.

Winston Churchill once said, 'Courage is what it takes to stand up and speak. Courage is also what it takes to sit down and listen'. Listening is both the most powerful and the least utilised of all communication tools. Learn to use it well, and watch the impact it has on your relationships. Your ears will never get you into trouble.

Train the brave

If you want to be listened to, begin by doing some listening! Think of someone you've not seen eye to eye with and organise a time to catch up. Enter the conversation with no agenda except to understand what they think, why they think that and how they feel about it.

Listen with your intuition, not only to what they're saying, but to what they aren't. Be open to the possibility that they have something of great value for you. Then notice the impact you've made — on them, on yourself, on the future. That alone will be worth your time.

CHAPTER 16

Be willing to rock the boat

In my 'first career' I landed what I thought was a pretty plum job working in marketing for a large multinational. It had been pitched as a really important position, with a lot of exciting opportunities for me to really make my mark. To my dismay, within a couple months of arriving I disovered the reality was very different. I found myself working in a very dysfunctional team with a manager who was clearly either going through a mid-life crisis or just more focused on other things outside our department. I suspect both. Day after day I would show up and try to make my mark on the role with close to no direction and zero feedback.

As the months passed, I found myself increasingly disillusioned. By the time I was nearing a year in the role I decided I could bear it no longer and began looking for a new position outside the company. At the exit interview with the department director, he asked me why I was leaving. I decided I had nothing to lose and may as well be candid with him. To my surprise he conveyed sincere disappointment and then asked why I hadn't spoken up earlier to share my concerns as he would have appreciated the opportunity to have addressed them. The truth was, I was simply too timid to rock the boat and too afraid of the fallout. The lesson was an important one. When we cower from addressing issues for fear of rocking the boat, we sell out on ourselves and can end up being rocked out of it anyway.

When I look back on some of the not-so-pleasant experiences in my career and relationships, on every single occasion I can identify where I held back from confronting an issue when I shouldn't have because I was afraid someone might think I was being difficult, hard to get along with, uncooperative or pushy. I was trying to be a nice person — agreeable and easy to work with. Alas, I was trying too hard.

CHALLENGING THE NORM CAN BE RISKY, BUT NO LESS THAN BEING OVERLY AGREEABLE.

I like nice people. Who doesn't, right? But, like every virtue, too much niceness can have a downside. Of course, being agreeable, affable and amenable is often a great thing, helping you to build trusting and rewarding relationships. Likewise, no-one likes someone who is forever forcing their opinion, constantly argumentative and overly demanding. However, if you're not willing to push back from time to time, you can find yourself feeling increasingly resentful and frustrated, and unable to accomplish what you want.

Ita Buttrose once shared with me that the world would be a very dull place if no-one ever rocked the boat. Likewise, if all you ever do is 'go along to get along' you'll sometimes diminish yourself and deprive others of the impact you'd make by speaking up and putting forward your opinion, even if it ruffles the odd feather. Sure, there'll be people who won't always agree with you. Some may think you're being a pain in the butt. Criticism and confrontation may ensue. However, in today's workplace where 'yes-men' (and women) who are quick to take the safe option can seem all too plentiful, those who are willing to speak their mind — courteously, but candidly — not only add more value, but become more valued by those around them. As Margaret Thatcher once said, 'If you set out to be liked, you will accomplish nothing'.

How to push back without being pushy

There is both an art and a science to knowing how to push back without coming across as pushy. Here are five suggestions to help you do just that.

1. Don't make people wrong

If you've ever had someone challenge your opinion, even gently, you'll have experienced how quickly it can make you feel defensive, as though you were under personal attack (even if you intellectually knew you weren't!). Likewise, if what you have to say may be threatening to others, be very clear in distinguishing between the opinion you're pushing back against and the person who holds it. When people perceive that you're trying to put them down or lay blame, they instinctively go into the defensive. So instead of saying 'yes, but . . .', say 'yes, and . . .'. The former may come across as combative while the latter acknowledges their view as valid and invites further discussion.

2. Enquire before advocating

We all like to think our way of seeing things is the right way. So before you try to convince someone otherwise, take time to understand how they came to see things as they do. This moves you from advocating for your opinion to enquiring about theirs. When people sense you're genuinely trying to understand their perspective, they become more receptive to yours.

(continued)

How to push back without being pushy *(cont'd)*

3. Start with what you both care about

Whether it's a mutual concern for the bottom line or the state of your relationship, make sure you frame your opinion in the context of what you both care about. That way, people won't see you as arguing *against* them as much as trying to work *with* them to create a better outcome. It can subtly shift the emotional space from being combative to collaborative.

4. Arm yourself with solutions, not complaints

It's easy to complain. It's why so many people excel at it. It's not so easy to find a practical solution that takes care of everyone's (not just your own) concerns. So whenever you can, come armed with a suggestion that addresses the issue, along with examples of where your idea has worked for others. Since most people tend towards risk-averseness, sharing how others have been successful in similar situations can lessen misgivings and increase buy-in. If you have no solution, then enlist their support in finding one.

5. Know when to let it rest

You won't always get others to see things your way so know when to let it go and move on. At least now people know where you stand and you can either accept things as they are or make other plans. Either way, you'll have built self-respect for making a stand and likely also earned the respect of those you challenged for the courage it took you to do so.

Train the brave

Saying something that rubs against the consensus opinion can cause friction. However, being too agreeable when you need to speak assertively can put your self-respect at risk. How is your fear of rocking the boat (and being regarded as bossy or pushy or even difficult to get along with) keeping you from speaking up more bravely?

[illegible]

Sometimes letting [illegible] However [illegible] when you need to speak assertively [illegible] your self- [illegible] being [illegible] up more brave [illegible]

CHAPTER 17
Talk more; type less

After 14 months of marriage, actor Russell Brand sent a text message to pop star Katy Perry to say he wanted a divorce. While I'm sure he was very busy that day, I would have thought he could have spared a few minutes to give her a call. Or maybe I'm just old fashioned!

As revolutionising as technology has been in our lives, it's also become an all-too-convenient way of avoiding the real work of meaningful communication when it matters most. Whether discussing something that's upset us, or letting someone know we want to end a relationship, our innate aversion to confrontation combined with the sheer convenience of digital communication drives people to typing when they really should be talking.

OUR DEVICES CATER TO COWARDICE. DON'T HIDE BEHIND ONE JUST BECAUSE YOU CAN.

Too often we take the easy, and often cowardly, option of hiding behind our digital devices — email, text messaging or social media — rather than braving the raw discomfort of either picking up the phone or, better still, sitting down and having a good old-fashioned face-to-face conversation. Indeed, when it comes to having an awkward or difficult conversation, nothing can ever replace a real, face-to-face, human-to-human conversation. So while texting, instant messaging and emailing are brilliant tools for communicating efficiently, they can be very blunt ones when used inappropriately. Ask Katy.

NOTHING REPLACES REAL, OLD-FASHIONED-STYLE CONVERSATION.

Not long ago, a woman I know sent a text message to a friend of hers to say she'd decided she didn't want to go on a joint family holiday together. She and her husband had talked it over and decided they didn't think the kids would get along. This woman later shared with me that her friend had not taken it well and a lengthy text exchange had ensued that left both women feeling bruised and estranged from each other. If only this were a one-off sort of situation; but it isn't.

I regularly see adults — 'digital immigrants' such as myself — resorting to lengthy text exchanges rather than picking up the phone. Sure, sometimes it may be the most efficient way to communicate, but often it's because it can feel less threatening than a personal conversation. Which is why, as a parent of four 'digital natives', I think it's really important to encourage my kids not to live their lives online, but to practise the art of conversation. After all, the more often you opt to type rather than talk, the less practice you get building the skills and confidence required to engage in the often difficult conversations vital to building strong relationships and navigating conflict. And while tapping away on your smartphone may seem smart, in the longer term it can be anything but, exacting a profound price on your relationships; your ability to influence, lead, manage conflict and build collaboration; and the health of your heart.

Five times to talk before you type

While there's no set of rules for when to talk versus when to type, there are situations when choosing the latter can damage trust and only make situations worse. Here are five times you should step away from your device and choose talking over texting.

1. When there's a good chance of being misunderstood

While a masterful poet may be able to convey emotion accurately through the written word, the rest of us tend to do a less proficient job, and the emotion we intend to convey gets lost in translation. The source of the problem deals directly with emotion — the emotion you're writing with and the one being read with can be starkly different. As soon as you begin using text phrases to characterise emotion that would normally be delivered with vocal intonation, subtle nuances, facial expressions and body language, your intended message can be completely misconstrued.

If the person you're writing to is particularly sensitive about an issue, they'll be even more prone to putting a negative spin on your words. You can spare yourself the damage control by taking extra time up front to pick up the phone or meet in person to ensure the other person hears your message in the most positive way.

2. When you're angry

Sending an email to someone when you're red-raging mad is almost guaranteed not to end well. I have a 'sleep on it' rule myself. While I may compose an email just to have a good vent, I never even type the name of the recipient lest I accidentally press 'send'. Instead,

(continued)

Five times to talk before you type *(cont'd)*

I file it as a draft and either sleep on it or give myself at least two hours to cool my jets before rewriting and pressing 'send'. Without exception, I always soften my tone, include more pleasantries and remove the heated language that's guaranteed to raise defences.

3. When bowing out of a commitment

If you have to bow out of a commitment such as dinner plans (or going on a holiday with someone), making a call can simply be an act of courtesy that shows you respect the dignity of the other person, even if you're no longer able, or you don't want to, hang out with them. And, needless to say, if you're ending a relationship (much less a marriage), have the guts to *say* it, not *send* it.

4. When you're apologising

For an apology to hold any water, the person you're making it to needs to feel your sincerity. Apologising via text may be fine if you forgot to drop off the dry cleaning, but it can show a lack of genuine remorse for almost anything else. Picking up the phone or saying sorry in person also provides the valuable opportunity to ask for forgiveness, see if there's anything you can do to make amends and restore any ill feeling in the relationship.

5. When you're criticising

Delivering criticism in a way that others can take onboard isn't easy at the best of times. Using email to deliver it exponentially increases the factor of difficulty. Sitting behind your computer screen unable to see someone's emotional reaction can give you a false sense of bravado that desensitises you to how they're really feeling. Because you can't see their hurt, you care less about it. All the while your written words strip what you say of nuance and emotional tone.

While criticising someone via email may be less confronting for you, it leaves you wide open to causing enormous injury to your relationship, which will take far more time to repair than any time saved by firing off a quick email. Providing feedback in person enables you to read visual cues, tread gently when needed, clarify misunderstandings and immediately address issues as they arise.

Next time you're tempted to fire off a quick typed message in a moment of anger or frustration, guilt, regret or plain old laziness, ask yourself whether email is truly the best medium or just the most comfortable. In today's era of communication cowardice, having the courage to brave a 'real conversation' can make a profound difference to the quality of the relationships you build, the influence you grow and, as ironic as it may seem, your communication efficiency!

Likewise, if you think about the people in your life who you care about, consider how making a phone call, rather than sending an email, might make them feel. Too often, we send emails and texts back and forth to people in our lives because it's more convenient and efficient rather than picking up the phone to say hello and find out how they're doing. With friends scattered across multiple timezones around the world, it's easy to go long periods of time without actually speaking. But every now and again I'll pick up the phone and make a call. The delight in people's voices when they hear my voice always makes me smile, and the conversations we have are nearly always much richer than anything we convey via email.

So, whether it's a difficult conversation you'd rather avoid, or simply a way of conveying how much people mean to you, nothing can ever trump the power of the spoken word.

Train the brave

Where have you been hiding behind the safety of your screen to avoid the real, and sometimes uncomfortable, work of communication? Who would you talk to today if you were being courageous or simply wanted to make the extra effort to show how much you care? Go on ... be brave. Notice the difference it makes.

CHAPTER 18

Hold people accountable

'He often misses deadlines.'

'I'm always having to chase her on things.'

'He's perpetually late.'

If you've ever found yourself frustrated at someone who's perpetually slack, late or unreliable, you'll relate to some of the comments above. Many people value their promises cheaply or simply manage their commitments poorly. Others have a hard time holding people to account. It's easier to just let it go, do it yourself and hope they'll be more reliable next time. The problem is, they rarely are.

It's an old rule of life that we teach people how to treat us. Accordingly, if you don't hold people accountable when they fail to follow through on commitments, you're implicitly condoning the behaviour. But, like so many of the things you know are good for you to do, holding people accountable requires exiting your comfort zone. It's why it takes an ounce or two of courage. Sometimes more.

YOU GET WHAT YOU TOLERATE.

Whether you're managing a business of 5000 or your life of one, when you don't call people on their broken promises and ill-managed commitments, you become part of the problem. By letting things slide — perhaps by doing them yourself — you're inadvertently teaching them that their behaviour is acceptable. The one thing you can count on is to expect more of it. More broken promises. More turning up late. More cut corners. More excuses. More missed deadlines. More shoddy work. And along with these, more frustration, mistrust, stress and resentment.

Turning the tide begins with making a commitment to managing your own pledges with integrity — doing what you say you'll do when you say you'll do it — and then expecting no less from others. Failing to manage accountability in the commitments you make to others, and those made to you, has a ripple effect that's far-reaching and costly. It doesn't just undermine your own integrity, reputation and influence, it impacts everyone around you.

How to hold people accountable

You teach people how to treat you and how to regard the commitments they make to you. Ignoring the times when people treat commitments cheaply sets you up for more of the same. And it doesn't serve them either! So, if you're overdue a conversation about accountability, here are four steps to help you on your way (and a lesson on getting your kids to tidy their room!).

1. Ensure everyone is clear about what's expected

When my daughter Maddy was about six I went upstairs to check that she'd cleaned her room as she'd promised. When I walked in, I was pleasantly surprised by what a great job she'd done. And then I opened her wardrobe door. Out toppled everything that had been scattered around her bedroom floor: barbies, books, art supplies, tea sets, dried paint pallets, princess dresses, dirty clothes, a wet towel, her brother's fire truck, dried apple cores and gum wrappers. Needless to say, it was then that I realised I hadn't been sufficiently explicit in clarifying my idea of 'clean'. As far as she was concerned, she'd done a great job!

Sometimes you can clear up a simple misunderstanding at the outset just by clarifying what it was you expected in the first place. To ensure against the same thing happening again, always make sure people are clear about both *what* you expect to be done and *when* you expect it to be done. Ambiguity is a recipe for frustration and unmet expectation.

2. Seek an explanation before making an accusation

It's always important to give someone the benefit of the doubt to begin with. Maybe they've just been really busy and thought other priorities were more important. Maybe they needed more guidance. Maybe something came up out of the blue and they just forgot to tell you. Hear them out and give them a chance to explain themselves.

3. Share the impact

People aren't always conscious of how their behaviour impacts other people, or even themselves. So you need to be straight with them about how their failure to do what they said, when they said, has impacted you, others and them! Maybe you had to work back late to finish what they didn't. Maybe it affected your entire team and

(continued)

How to hold *people* accountable *(cont'd)*

you had to manage the fallout. Maybe you're just disappointed with them. Maybe you'll have to think twice before relying on them again. Maybe others will. Maybe you'll need to engage others to do their job until trust is restored (assuming it can be). This isn't about making them feel bad; it's just being upfront about the impact so you can make things better in the future.

4. Reset expectations

After telling Maddy that I wasn't nearly as jubilant with the state of her room as she clearly was, I got down on my knees beside Maddy and together we began sorting through the pile that had fallen out of her wardrobe. The dress-ups go in the dress-up box; the apple core and wrappers into the bin; the truck back to her brother's room; the books neatly onto the shelf. Simple stuff, but an important exercise for us both. That said, she's now a teenager and I no longer hold her accountable for her room. She's now old enough to take ownership of doing that herself and I've stopped caring so much! Likewise, if someone has let you down it's important to renegotiate exactly what it is you want, when you want it and what they're able to deliver. By having the courage to have the conversation, rather than tip-toeing around, you set the stage for greater accountability and less disappointment.

While I was running a workshop with a group of leaders in law enforcement, a fairly tough-looking man who'd spent his career investigating organised crime shared how holding people in his department accountable was one of the most difficult aspects of his job. 'I just find it stressful and so often just put it off,' he confided to me and his colleagues in the room. Many nodded. I found it ironic that this group of men and women, who spent their lives dealing with hardcore criminals and investigating homicides, organised crime and major fraud, found having personal conversations with their colleagues about what they had or hadn't done one of the more difficult aspects of their job. It just goes to show that sometimes it's the seemingly small issues that, left untended, can cause us the most frustration and call for the greatest courage.

So, as uncomfortable as you may feel, just know that when you do what you know is right and hold people accountable to their word, everyone — including them — is ultimately better off. (Just don't expect a thank-you card.)

Train the brave

Where have you been avoiding holding someone accountable for a broken promise (or a series of them)? The temporary awkwardness you may feel by addressing the issue will be far outweighed by the ongoing cost you'll pay if you don't.

CHAPTER 20

Offer feedback; it's an act of service

Hillary Clinton once said, 'It is important to learn how to take criticism seriously but not personally'. It's excellent advice, but if you've ever been criticised (and let's face it, who hasn't?) you'll know that it's easier said than done, even when it's given in the gentlest of ways with the best of intentions. That's because hearing critical feedback strikes at the heart of two core human needs — the need to learn and grow, and the need to be accepted just the way we are. Consequently, even a gentle suggestion to do something differently can leave us feeling wounded. Encouragement not to 'take it personally' often does little to soften the blow.

Yet, as Hillary Clinton, a woman who's had more criticism directed her way than most people, has also said, 'Critics can be your best friends if you listen to them, and learn from them, but don't get dragged down by them'. Learning to do that is as important to your growth and success in work and life as your willingness to offer others constructive feedback is to theirs.

NOT GIVING CONSTRUCTIVE FEEDBACK DEPRIVES PEOPLE OF A CHANCE TO BETTER THEMSELVES.

Many people are extremely reluctant to offer critical feedback. It's because we're so uncomfortable with the emotions that can arise from it — our own and others'. We hate to cause offence and we loathe hurting other people's feelings or inciting resentment, which only exacerbates existing issues. The safer option is to simply say nothing, let people continue on as they are, and just hope they'll eventually realise how their behaviour is hurting them and impacting others. But problematic behaviours that may seem obvious to you are rarely obvious to the person exhibiting them. Let's face it, if it were easy to see how our actions limited our success we'd be more proactive in changing them!

Which is why, if you can see that someone is acting in a way that limits their success, you do them a profound disservice if you shy away from giving them feedback for fear of causing offence. Of course, that's not to say you should walk around dishing out your version of 'constructive criticism' all day (as self-satisfying as that may be!). After all, if people have no regard for what you have to say, it wastes everyone's time. However, whether it's someone you're managing or someone you simply care about seeing do better, integrity calls you to stop playing so safe and to lay your own comfort on the line for the sake of the good your feedback might do.

Feedback should never be given lightly and must always be delivered considerately, with the highest of intentions for the person you're giving it to. The reality is that it's extremely easy to be critical of people. Many people excel at it and spend their lives offering up unsolicited and unwanted critiques of everyone. It's not so easy to be critical in a way that people can accept without offence, act on positively and ultimately be thankful for.

BE HONEST ABOUT YOUR MOTIVATIONS BEFORE OFFERING FEEDBACK. ONLY GIVE IT WHEN YOU'RE SURE OF HOW IT WILL SERVE THE PERSON RECEIVING IT.

So, before you open your mouth to offer feedback, take time to get really clear about *why* you want to give it and *how* doing so will provide a genuine service to the person you're giving it to. What comes from the heart lands on the heart. Criticism that comes from fear — or the fear-related emotions of insecurity, defensiveness, anxiety, anger, jealousy or pride — is guaranteed not to land well and will only trigger similar emotions in others. Sure, you may get something off your chest, vent your frustration and put someone back in their place, but at what cost to trust, integrity, performance and your future relationship?

When it comes to actually delivering the feedback, it's important to focus on the behaviour you want to see more of, rather than the behaviour you're hoping will change. You can do this with my simple, four-step ACED model. (Don't you love acronyms!) Hopefully it will help you ace your feedback next time you feel compelled to give it.

The ACED feedback formula

Everyone likes to receive praise and few people enjoy being criticised. Most of us find it hard not to take constructive feedback personally, at least a little bit, no matter how much praise we may get each side of it. But that doesn't mean you shouldn't give people the opportunity to better themselves. By telling someone

(continued)

The ACED feedback formula *(cont'd)*

'You did a great job', or 'I didn't like that report', you're not giving them anything they can work with to improve themselves. Based on factual observations, not personal feelings, constructive feedback addresses specific issues and concerns that help people become aware of how they could improve.

ASK for permission

No-one enjoys hearing feedback about what they aren't doing well, but they'll take it on better if you first ask if they'd like to receive it. Just ask, 'Can I share some feedback with you that I hope will be helpful?' This simple question can reframe your words from being about you making a judgement to you trying to be helpful. When my client Lisa actively sought feedback, she asked for three specific things she could do better. Doing so made it safer for others to be candid with her. By asking for permission to give feedback, you make it safer for the person hearing it.

Specify the context and CURRENT behaviour

Be specific in describing the current behaviour you want to give feedback on. Provide context by defining the 'where' and 'when' of the recent situation you're referring to. Just don't waffle on. Be clear, concise and come armed with recent examples to illustrate what you're talking about. For example, 'During this morning's meeting, when you gave your presentation . . .'

Explain the EFFECT of the behaviour

Most of us aren't fully aware of how we 'show up' for those around us. Hearing that people find us abrupt or unfocused, difficult or disorganised can feel like a punch in the gut. So go gently in sharing the effect that you see someone's behaviour has on you and other people and how it can impact their future. Make sure they understand why it's in their best interest to listen to your feedback and act on it accordingly. If they don't see how their behaviour is actually hurting them, it will be hard to motivate them to change it.

Describe the DESIRED behaviour

Finally, state the behaviour you'd like to see more of. The more specific you can be, the better! Here are a couple examples of these steps in action:

'When you cut me off in meetings (*context and current behaviour*), I feel undermined (*effect on you*). I also feel it comes across as abrasive to others (*effect on others*). In the future, I'd appreciate it if you let me finish what I'm saying before you share your opinion (*desired behaviour*).'

'When you constantly check your phone while we're out together like you did at dinner last night (*context and current behaviour*), I feel like you'd rather be somewhere else than with me (*effect on you*). I also feel it's rude to the people we're out with (*effect on others*). From now on, I'd appreciate it if you'd turn your phone off, or at least put it away, when we're with company (*desired behaviour*).'

GIVING CRITICAL FEEDBACK ALWAYS INVOLVES RISK AND INVITES COURAGE.

Withholding feedback that could help someone be more successful deprives them of an invaluable opportunity to better themselves. Sure, people may not always like what you have to say. They may not even agree with you. However, by not giving them the opportunity to hear what's on your mind—and how their behaviour impacts you, others and their own future—you're doing everyone a profound disservice.

There's no fail-safe way to give critical feedback. It's why so many don't. What if they burst into tears? What if they start screaming insults at you? What if they quit their job or accuse you of bullying? Yes, they're all risks you have to take. But when you park your ego and enter into a conversation clear on how you intend to help, you can trust in the knowledge that you ultimately will help. Surely that's worth the risk.

Train the brave

Shakespeare once wrote, 'No legacy is so rich as honesty'. Giving critical feedback requires you to be more committed to the potential upside for the person you're giving it to than to the potential downside for you. Don't let fear of an awkward conversation keep you from sharing feedback that could help them do better and be better. Is there someone you could help today by offering them a few considered, kind—yet candid—words of feedback?

CHAPTER 21

Say sorry even when it's difficult

I've had many humbling parenting moments in my life. One of the ones etched deepest in my memory was the time I lost my temper with my daughter Maddy, who was four at the time. We were in a crowded Dallas shopping mall on a cold January day and Maddy had been at me (and at me and at me) to take her to the Disney store. I'd said no again (and again and again). I had my two sons in tow who were both hungry and we needed to eat, not browse Snow White dresses. On top of that, I was seven months pregnant with number four, weary and still jetlagged from a long flight back from Australia just days before. The last thing I felt like doing was going to the Disney store. But Maddy was four, she *loooooved* princesses, adored Snow White and couldn't … ah, make that *wouldn't*! … take no for an answer.

As we made our way to a table in the middle of a busy food court, I finally cracked. I turned to my curly-haired little girl and, in a voice far louder than I'd planned, shouted 'Can. You. Just. SHUT. UP!' At which point, Maddy promptly burst into tears. My never-loses-his-cool husband Andrew looked over at me and gave me a look as if to say, 'If we were at home right now I'd be putting you in time out'. I felt ashamed. I felt embarrassed. I'd clearly lost my temper at my beautiful daughter and done the very thing I admonish my kids for — being unkind. Not only that, but every person within ear shot (which was a lot of people at 12 pm in a food court on a wintery Saturday) was looking at me as if to say, 'Shame on you!'

Feeling two feet tall, I bent over to Maddy, wiped the tears rolling down her rosy cheek and took her hand. 'Maddy, I'm sorry. I lost my temper. I shouldn't have done that and I'm very sorry. What can I do to make it up to you?' At which she pointed directly at the nearby Baskin-Robbins counter. Ah, the way to a four-year-old's heart.

Just when I thought the whole humiliating episode was over, Lachlan, who was nearly five at the time, looked at me with great earnestness and said, 'Mummy, you lost your temper? That's bad isn't it?'

'Yes, it is,' I said, growing more ashamed with each passing moment. 'I shouldn't have lost my temper.' And then, with childish innocence and heart-warming industriousness he put his hands on his hips and, announced, 'Well, we better go and find it!'

It was a priceless and poignant moment. Needless to say, I did not find my temper in 'Lost & Found', but after some self-imposed 'time out' and a good night's sleep.

SORRY IS HARDEST WHEN IT MATTERS MOST.

I don't share that story to expose my shortfalls as a parent. (My children will happily tell you I have many!) Rather, because it's probably one of the easier times I've had to fall on my sword and apologise over the years. The harder times have been apologising to a friend for being insensitive, to my husband for being self-centred and to my employees for being indecisive or failing to provide the direction they needed.

Saying a quick sorry when you bump into someone is pretty easy. Saying sorry when you've put self-interest ahead of doing what's right can be anything but. To be truly meaningful, an apology must not only come from the heart, it must be backed up with a solid intention not to repeat the behaviour and to make amends for what you did.

I am sorry. I did the wrong thing. I hope you can forgive me. How can I make it up?

Of course, it's often impossible to restore things to how they once were. But even then, just doing what you can to make amends can make a big difference. Not just to the person you may have wronged, but to yourself. As author Craig Silvey wrote in his novel *Jasper Jones*, 'Sorry means you feel the pulse of other people's pain as well as your own, and saying it means you take a share of it ... Sorry doesn't take things back, but it pushes things forward. It bridges the gap'.

NEVER RUIN YOUR APOLOGY WITH AN EXCUSE.

There are often occasions when we need to say sorry not because we intentionally did anything wrong, but because our actions unintentionally caused hurt, harm or inconvenience. Just because you didn't mean to cause injury doesn't negate the need to apologise for it. Saying you're sorry lets people know you care, even if you'd do the same thing again. So don't undermine your apology by making excuses and justifications. If you can't apologise sincerely, say nothing lest you just add insult to injury.

SORRY TAKES COURAGE, BUT SAYING IT CLEANS THE SLATE FOR YOU TO ACCESS SO MUCH MORE.

Many people have a hard time saying they're sorry, or admitting they messed up or acted thoughtlessly. That's because saying sorry makes you feel vulnerable and lays bare your fallibility and shortcomings, your selfishness and insensitivity. While in the short term it's easy to skirt around your failings, over time it can build wedges in your relationships and cracks in your life. Sure, you can try to minimise and justify your wrongdoing, or the unintended consequences of your actions, but you carry them with you nonetheless. Saying sorry takes courage, but by acting with it you clean the slate that keeps you from accessing so much more.

There's little more healing than being able to put the past in the past. When you say sorry, seek forgiveness and work to clean up any mess that's resulted, you free up your future to live better, act kinder and enjoy more authentic relationships. Sorry bridges the gap between a past that can't be changed and a future that's yet to be made. 'Sorry' is an offering, a sacrament, a gift. It's not making yourself wrong for being human; it's acknowledging you did wrong but are committed to doing better. As Wayne Dyer once said, 'True nobility isn't about being better than anybody else, but being better than you used to be'. Learning how to say sorry liberates you to do just that.

Train the brave

Saying sorry and being sorry are not the same sorry. So take a moment to think about times you may have caused someone hurt or injury that you never apologised for. How might having the courage to say sorry and seeking to make amends lighten your load and expand your future?

Part III
Work passionately

How to risk the bravery your potential is counting on

CHAPTER 22
Work as though what you do matters; it does

A few years ago my friend Caren Merrick decided to stop lamenting the lack of businesswomen like herself in the state legislature and to run for the Virginia state senate. Over the 12 months prior to election day, Caren worked hard raising funds, knocking on doors (10 000 of them!) and learning about the concerns of those she hoped to represent. Week after week, she gave up weeknights and weekends with her family to earn the votes she needed to win. Midway through her campaign, her electoral district was redrawn and she found herself running in a new district that had voted for the opposing party for more than 30 years. While Caren knew the odds of winning were stacked against her, she decided the work she was doing was too important not to continue. So she pressed on, giving her all with even greater resolve.

Countless times Caren had to step outside her comfort zone, confront people who disagreed with her views and make herself vulnerable to the uglier side of politics, the name calling and smearing. On election day I offered to open our home to her supporters. As the vote count started to come in, our hopes began to grow thin. By early evening they were petering out altogether and I worried how Caren would handle the disappointment. I shouldn't have. The moment she walked out to the crowd assembled in my living room I just knew she'd be okay. Not because she hadn't wanted to win (she hadn't worked her tail off to lose!), but because her belief in her cause was more important than the outcome of her efforts. Winning or losing would not define her; only her commitment to giving her very best to a worthy endeavour. Caren began her concession speech with a quote by Teddy Roosevelt that encapsulated her mindset; one that I committed to memory that night and have been inspired by ever since:

> ***Far and away the best prize that life has to offer is the chance to work hard at work worth doing.***

OUR WORK ISN'T JUST A MEANS TO MAKE A LIVING; OUR WORK IS A MEANS TO MAKE OURSELVES.

One of the most dangerous risks people take is spending the best and most productive years of their lives doing something for which they hold no passion on the bet that they can buy themselves the freedom to do it later. It rarely works out that way. Sure, there are people in the world who truly have no choice about the work they do. But odds are you're not one of them. And while you may not always feel you're in a position to change what you do (at least not in the short term), you always have a choice in how you approach it. *Always.*

Work is often something we think of as a tiresome chore we 'have' to do to get by. Yet work is so much more than that — it's not just a means to making a living, it's a means to making yourself. It's not just good for your finances; it's good for your soul. As Pope Paul VI once said, 'The very striving and hard work that we so constantly try to avoid is the major building block in the person we are today'. Indeed, it's through sheer old hard work that we grow the confidence and competence to thrive in our lives outside work.

IF YOU DISLIKE YOUR WORK, EITHER CHANGE WHAT YOU DO OR CHANGE HOW YOU DO IT.

I regularly meet people living in a constant state of resentment or indifference towards their job. Employee surveys show that about two-thirds of people go to work each day believing that what they feel doesn't really matter. Sure, they get their job done (sort of), but their care factor is low and their attitude indifferent at best. The economic cost of disengagement runs in the billions, but the cost to the human spirit is immeasurable.

While few people relish every moment or aspect of their job, there's little more tragic than the choice millions of people make to stay in jobs or professions from which they draw no — or little — satisfaction. It's why I passionately believe that if you don't like what you do, you either need to change what you do or change how you approach it. Anything less makes you complicit in your unhappiness.

BETTER TO FAIL AT DOING WORK YOU LOVE THAN SUCCEED DOING WORK YOU LOATHE.

One of the biggest challenges most of us face in bringing our best selves to work is our attachment to the outcomes we want to achieve. Of course, detaching from an outcome is far easier said than done, but genuine success in life is not about whether you always achieve the goals and outcomes you want (whether it's winning a seat in public office or penning a bestseller). It's having the courage to press on when the going gets tough while holding onto your belief in the importance of what you're doing. Far better to be a failure at something you love than a success at something you loathe.

It takes courage to keep faith in the importance of what you do, particularly when those around you appear not to. It's so easy to get pulled into the comparison trap, wanting to feel that you're 'beating' (or at least keeping up with) those around you. But measuring your value by external markers that stroke your ego but don't feed your spirit — whether it's the car you drive, the status of your position or the prestigious awards that earn you status — can take a toll. Yes, those 'gold star' markers may affirm your significance to others, but at what cost to your heart's deepest longing? As Richard Branson has said, 'There is no greater thing you can do with your life and your work than follow your passions — in a way that serves the world and you'.

WORK HARD. BE PATIENT. THE REST WILL FOLLOW.

'Sure, sure,' I hear people say, 'it's all well and good to say, "Follow your passion", but what about when life's responsibilities and realities don't make that an option?' To which I often say, 'Then be passionate about giving your best to whatever job you're in'. I also love to share one of my favourite quotes by Mother Teresa: 'Not all of us can do great things. But we can do small things with great love'.

I once heard a story about a management consultant who was engaged to do some work at a large cancer hospital. Upon meeting someone working as a janitor he asked them, 'Tell me about what you do here'. Without hesitation the janitor replied, 'I help to cure cancer'. The story stuck with me because it revealed the truth that *every single job holds value,* however small or seemingly insignificant you (or others) perceive your role to be. Likewise, when you talk yourself down (which most of us do too often — particularly us women!) or talk your job down, you diminish yourself and undermine the value that you bring.

HARD WORK DOESN'T GUARANTEE SUCCESS, BUT YOU CAN'T SUCCEED WITHOUT IT.

A few months ago I attended the funeral of one of my dad's dearest friends, Alec, who had passed away after a long battle with prostate cancer. Like my dad, Alec had been a dairy farmer his entire life. He had worked long hours, weathered droughts and all manner of hardships to raise his six children. As I arrived at the church for his funeral, it was absolutely packed as people poured in to pay their respects. My dad gave the eulogy and Alec's children shared fond memories before the priest shared his admiration for Alec, saying that while he may have lived a very simple and ordinary life he did so with extraordinary love, faith, kindness and character. His words struck a chord as they spoke to the heart of what truly matters most in life — not what we do or accomplish, not the wealth we accrue or the status we gain, but how we do it and the small ways we impact those around us along the way.

Hard work — whether raising a family (the hardest job of all), serving cafeteria meals, sorting frozen corn cobs or selling incontinence bed sheets (all jobs I've done over the years!) — is *always* work worth doing. Not simply for what you get, but because of who you become in the process: more skilled, more grateful, more valued and more valuable.

Albert Einstein wrote that doing one's best is a sacred responsibility. And so, regardless of the work you do right now, the success you've achieved or the lack thereof, recommit yourself to giving the very best you have and then trust that, whatever happens, that will be enough. Because more important than what you may achieve is the person you become by showing up at work each day (particularly when you're most tempted not to) and daring to believe that what you do makes a difference. It does.

Train the brave

Where might you be failing to give your best and show up fully because you discount the value of the work that you do? What do you need to change about *what* you do or *how* you approach it so that you can honour yourself and your potential to make a more significant difference?

CHAPTER 23
Play to win, not to avoid losing

On the day of the 2014 World Cup final in Brazil my three sons set the alarm at 4.45 am so they could watch the game from our home in Australia. They woke me soon after. 'You can't miss this one, Mum!' they announced ripping the covers off my bed. As we sat around in our pyjamas, cups of tea in hand, we were all gunning for Argentina and waiting for Lionel Messi, their star player, to have his much anticipated 'Maradona moment'.

Alas, it never came. When Germany finally scored the one and only game-winning goal with a few minutes to play of the extended time, we had to reach for the tissues. And yes, it has to be said, 'I cried for Argentina'. While I'm not a particularly big soccer fan most of the time, I've grown to love the World Cup. The spectacle, the emotion, the anticipation, the elation of victory and the disappointing taste of defeat. There's plenty of it all.

Many times over the preceding month the commentators had expounded on whether a team was playing to win or playing not to lose. It struck me how well these two approaches describe the mindset many people bring to their career, business and life.

When you're playing not to lose, your focus isn't on what you could gain but on protecting what you already have. Your energies are channelled into shoring up the status quo and guarding against what you don't want to happen — whether that's a competitor eating into your market share or a colleague taking your job. While there's no doubt you need to be mindful about not losing turf you want to keep, being focused on protecting what you already have is driven by fear of what you don't want, rather than by ambition about what you do. It can take you into a vicious cycle from which it's hard to escape.

COURAGEOUS ACTION IS ALWAYS THE ULTIMATE CAREER MOVE.

Playing safe and avoiding risk often feels more secure and sensible in the short term. Yet while people are busily protecting what they have and doing the same thing they've always done, they run the risk of missing out on opportunities to try new things, to venture onto new ground and to seize opportunities. Instead of speaking up to add value at work, they stay quiet to avoid rocking the boat or endangering their position. But when their company starts restructuring, they're often less valued than those who have been exploring new ways of growing the business, who are willing to stick their necks out and who can be counted on for a candid opinion.

I've seen it happen to many people midway through their career when their hard work has brought them a measure of success, security and status. They've put in the hours to get to where they are. They know their industry inside out and can do their job blindfolded — at least most days. It's comfortable. It's secure. It's theirs and they'll be dammed if they're willing to put it at risk. So instead of shaking things up in their business to adapt to a changing market, investing time in building their skills, going after a new market or taking on a bigger role that they aren't guaranteed to nail, they stick with what they know, consolidating their power and trying to perfect what they already do well. Sometimes arrogance creeps in. They become complacent, closed-minded and resistant to anything new. Playing 'not to lose' — to shore up what they have — marks their approach to everything. But at what cost to their own growth and deepest fulfilment? At what cost to the long-term success of their career or business? At what cost to those who have to work with them? Even those who manage to retain their status and salary often live as a hostage to their ego, disconnected from passion and purpose.

It's not always easy to see where you may be playing not to lose, but if you're unhappy about where you are in any area of your life, or uninspired about the direction in which you're headed, then it's likely your current 'game plan' needs reworking. When you're playing to win, your energy is channelled into creating new opportunities, breaking new ground and going after what you want to make happen. It's about trading the safety of the known for the uncertainty of a future that's yet to be created. It requires putting what you already have at risk for the sake of something bigger, something better. It requires courage.

PLAYING SAFE CAN BE A HIGH-RISK STRATEGY. DON'T KID YOURSELF OTHERWISE.

While Lionel Messi missed out on his Maradona moment in the 2014 World Cup, it didn't take away from his supreme effort and that of his teammates, who played hard to win right up until that final whistle blew. Likewise, when you play to win in the bigger game of life you won't always kick the game-winning goal. Sometimes you'll fall short of the mark, and sometimes your risks won't pay off as you'd hoped. But you have to ask yourself what bigger prize you put at risk when you go through life focused only on protecting what you have, and avoiding any risk of failing or losing face.

If you only ever work to protect what you already have, you miss out on accomplishing what's still waiting to be done. To quote Helen Keller: 'Avoiding danger is no safer in the long run than outright exposure. The fearful are caught as often as the bold'. So play to win; not to avoid losing. In the bigger game of life, playing safe is often the most dangerous game plan of all.

Train the brave

German board-game designer Reiner Knizia once said, 'When playing a game, the goal is to win, but it is the goal that is important, not the winning'. Where do you need to be more proactive, bold and brave in going after something you really want, rather than playing safe and protecting or consolidating what you already have?

CHAPTER 24

Be the leader you would love to have

Sometimes when I'm running leadership programs in organisations, I ask people to put up their hand if they see themselves as a leader. It's always a good way for me to get a read of the room; to learn how many people perceive themselves in terms of their power, influence and ability to effect change.

Of course it's easier to feel like you're a leader if you're in a designated leadership role. It can be harder to feel like a leader if you aren't. But the reality is that everyone, regardless of their position, power or personality type, has the ability to lead others. All leadership begins within, by owning your power outwards to positively affect those around you.

I've met and worked with many people in senior positions of leadership over the years. Some have been quite charismatic, with a special way of making everyone around them feel valued. Others have been more introverted and less at home in a crowd. Some have been true visionaries; others happier in the details.

What sets the best leaders apart isn't their superior intelligence, charismatic charm, a strategic mind or any of the other traits we often associate with leadership. It's who they are as human beings: authentic, purposeful, trustworthy, unpretentious, reflective and courageous in their own way. Yes, they have healthy egos, but they haven't been run by them. Yes, they are ambitious, but none are arrogant. And while they all hold positions of power, none are changed by it except to be even more purposeful in how they use it.

LEADERSHIP IS THE DOMAIN OF ANYONE WITH THE COURAGE TO ACT WITH IT.

The heart of leadership is not about formal power, status or strategic thinking. It's about making a choice to park your doubts and lay your reputation and sense of security on the line for a cause — whether a corporate vision or social value — that is bigger than yourself. Accordingly, all leadership begins with self-leadership. You can't hope to influence and create change in the world around you until you've taken on the hard work of creating change in the world within you. Likewise, it doesn't matter what position you hold or how impressive your résumé is (or not), your ability to positively influence others to do more, dream more and become more begins with your ability to do so yourself.

YOU LEAD BY VIRTUE OF WHO YOU ARE, NOT THE POSITION YOU HOLD.

You lead every time you let your imagination off the leash and connect with a vision that truly inspires you. You lead every time you set a bold course despite your misgivings. You lead every time you speak up about what's important to you. You lead every time you venture onto new ground. You lead every time you stick your neck out for what you believe in. You lead every time you do what's right over what's easy, particularly when it costs you. And you lead every time you encourage another person to expand their own horizon — to dare more, do more, give more and become more. And while people may not see you as a leader right away, when you consistently act like one you'll find they soon start to catch on.

WE AREN'T ALL MADE TO BE A CEO, BUT WE ARE ALL CALLED TO MAKE OUR MARK.

Great leaders don't get to be where they are because of the power they've been given, but because of how they used the power they've always had. The same power resides in you. Don't get me wrong though. Not everyone has what it takes to be CEO of a large multinational. But then, the vast majority of people wouldn't want to be! That's because we rarely aspire towards that for which we have little natural disposition. But each of us, regardless of our age, position or the authority bestowed upon us, can be a catalyst for positive change in our workplace, family, community, society and beyond. You are no exception.

DON'T WAIT TO BE TOLD YOU'RE A LEADER. ASSUME LEADERSHIP.

If you want to develop the quality of leadership, you must begin by acting as though you already have it. And so, whatever self-limiting story you have about yourself and your ability to lead, know this: *It's just a story*. Within you lies the ability to achieve significant and important things through the relationships you cultivate with others. But before you can lead others to higher ground, you must first lead yourself.

No-one will see you as a leader until you do. So don't wait to be made a leader; assume leadership. Not in an arrogant way. Not in a way that disrespects the position of others, but in a way that lets everyone know that you own your personal power, know your value and want to add more of it. Starting right now, park any old beliefs that limit your influence and admit to owning your innate power to effect positive change. Because, quite simply, that's what is at the heart of all leadership.

Train the brave

You don't need a title to be a leader. You don't need approval either. You just need the courage to step up to the plate and lead. So from today, walk as a leader, talk as a leader, think as a leader and act as a leader. Repeat again tomorrow. Over time your influence will spread. Try it!

CHAPTER 25

Quit quickly; fail fast

Surely persisting, persevering and not giving up, no matter what, is what it takes to achieve success in the bigger game of life? Sure. But in balance. While persistence is a hallmark of success, so too is knowing when to change the game plan, when to pull back and when to call it quits altogether. The irony is that by learning how to fail faster in the small things, you can set yourself up to succeed faster in the big.

Numerous times people have said to me something along the lines of, 'I can't quit now! Not when I've worked so hard. Not when I've sacrificed so much. It would all be for nothing!' To which I've often replied, 'Sure you can!' Sometimes calling it quits is exactly what you should do!

SOMETIMES CUTTING YOUR LOSSES IS THE BRAVEST (AND SMARTEST) THING TO DO.

There's a reason why smart people sometimes stay the course long after they should quit—whether sticking in a job, business, relationship or any situation. It's because of what psychologists have coined the 'Investment Trap'; that is, our aversion to losing (or 'wasting') what we've put into something compromises our judgement. This drives us to invest more when quitting and cutting our losses would serve us so much better. We just loathe the thought that we've wasted our time or money or energy, so we press on, even when logic would dictate us to do otherwise.

If you've ever kept reading a lousy book, or kept wearing an expensive but ill-fitting jacket just because you loathe to waste your hard-earned cash or precious time, you've fallen into the same trap. When you've invested a lot of yourself—financially, emotionally, socially, physically and mentally—into an endeavour, declaring it a mistake or failure is harder than pressing on ... at least in the short term. Changing the status quo is always painful, even if it's for the better. The question is:

How do you know when you should push on and when you shouldn't?

FAILURE IS AN EVENT, NOT A PERSON.

My friend Layne Beachley had to ask herself just this question. Layne's persistence and determination landed her six consecutive world surfing titles, making her the world's most successful female surfer. Even after suffering a career-ending neck injury, she couldn't call it quits for long and returned two years later to claim a seventh title, cementing her place in the record books. Layne then set her sights on launching her own clothing label. Her first swimwear line didn't take off, but she kept persisting. Again. And again. When her fifth attempt failed to get the traction it needed in a competitive market, Layne decided it was time to step back and reassess everything. She asked herself whether she had the right product, the right people, the right skills and the right amount of passion to make it work. It was 'no' on each count. So she asked herself, 'So why am I doing this?' Good question!

By answering honestly and bravely, Layne realised she needed to call it quits on her fashion label. As Layne shared with me during our interview for Raw Courage TV, 'It was really hard to walk away. I had to swallow my pride. But at the end of the day, I simply didn't have the passion and commitment needed to make it work'.

WINNERS DO QUIT. THEY JUST DON'T WASTE YEARS DOING IT.

'Winners never quit and quitters never win.' It's a well-worn saying, but it's not true. Whether it's a business venture that's not taking off, a promising job that's derailing, a rocky relationship or a bad investment, sometimes quitting is exactly what you need to do in order to move forward in your life and refocus your efforts on new endeavours, or on different paths, or using an alternative approach that will produce better results. Or, as Richie Norton says, 'Like creating a masterpiece, quitting is an art: you have to decide what to keep within the frame and what to keep out'.

IF YOU FIND YOURSELF IN A HOLE, STOP DIGGING.

Whether in our relationships, our work or other endeavours, too often we stay on the path we're on for the wrong reasons. We keep ploughing ahead not because we can see we're making steady progress in the direction we want to go, but because we're too proud to concede defeat and admit we got it wrong. So we double down, dig deeper, invest further and pray harder that if we just persist long enough and try hard enough, eventually our persistence will pay off. But doing more of something that's not working to begin with will only take us further in the wrong direction. So if you've invested down a path and it's not working out, don't keep doing the same thing in the vain (delusional!) hope that you'll suddenly land a different result. Hope is not a strategy. If you find yourself digging a hole, stop digging. It's a *loooong* way to see sunlight!

EVERY DAY YOU STICK TO SOMETHING THAT'S NOT WORKING IS A DAY YOU AREN'T WORKING ON SOMETHING THAT COULD.

A better approach to anything is to be ready to fail fast and not to let past mistakes shackle your future endeavours. Successful people have usually had far more failures than the average Joe because they're quick to acknowledge when they aren't onto a 'winner', to adjust, pivot and move on. They aren't ruled by their pride. They don't dwell on the failure itself. Nor do they cling to their plan, however clever they thought it was. Instead they learn the lessons and get to work on a new, and more informed, plan.

Every day you stick with something that's not working is a day you miss investing in something that could work. Soon after Layne closed down her retail brand she was invited to support the Australian team at the London Olympics. This was an opportunity she could never have seized had she been knee-deep building a retail line. As Layne learned, even when things don't work out to your original plan, there's always something really valuable to take you on your onward journey.

BE CAREFUL HOW YOU EXPLAIN YOUR FAILURES.

Failures provide invaluable stepping stones to future success, but only when you explain them in constructive ways. Martin Seligman, founder of a field of study called positive psychology, says you can predict a person's success after failure by their 'explanatory style'; that is, how they explain their failures. If you attribute your failure to factors you can't change, adjust or accommodate — whether internal or external — failure becomes a debilitating event. But if you attribute failure to something that's within your control to change or fix — a lack of knowledge that can be gained, systems that can be improved, skills that can be honed, strategies that can be reworked — you turn your failures into invaluable stepping stones. As basketballer Michael Jordan once said, 'I have failed over and over again in my life and that is why I succeed'.

YOU TRIED; IT DIDN'T WORK OUT. LEARN THE LESSON. MOVE ON.

Every great story of success is also one of great failure. Richard Branson, Steve Jobs and Donald Trump didn't hit the jackpot every time. Far from it. Rather, they risked failing again and again, and along the way learned a lot about what it takes to succeed. While you may never wish for failure, being willing to risk it is crucial. It's from your failures that you will grow the most, learn the most and achieve the most — if you approach them with the right attitude. So, if you want to succeed more, double your failure rate.

Winston Churchill once wrote, 'Never never give in, never give in, never, never, never'. He was right. And he was wrong. When it comes to moving towards the things that give you a sense of purpose, you should never quit. But that doesn't mean you shouldn't quit your current path and take a new one. Thomas Edison had 10 000 failures en route to inventing the light globe. So, if you're going to fail, fail fast. And if you're going to fall, fall forward. As Henry Ford once said, 'Failure is the opportunity to begin again more intelligently'. If you travelled in a car today, you'll be glad that he did just that.

Train the brave

All of life is an experiment. The more mistakes you make, the more you learn — about what works, and what doesn't. There's no shame in failing at something. What's most important is that you don't stick with something when it's clearly not leading towards the outcome you want. Where do you need to call it quits on something you've invested in so you can create the space for new possibilities?

CHAPTER 26
Never give anyone power to intimidate you

In my early twenties, when I began my (first) career working for a large oil company, I was completely intimidated by the director of sales and marketing. Bob was a good 20 years my senior and every time he passed by my pint-sized cubicle I'd get nervous and lose the power of speech (which, given how much I like to talk, is saying something!). One day, about six months into my job, I found myself seated beside Bob at a dinner. As Bob proceeded to engage in warm, friendly conversation it made me realise that my feeling of intimidation had nothing to do with Bob and everything to do with me.

That dinner taught me an important life lesson. People don't intimidate us ... rather, we allow people to intimidate us. That's not to say that some people don't act in ways intended to intimidate or diminish others. But in the end, it's not who they are being that creates our feelings of intimidation; it's the fact that we aren't secure and strong enough in our worth that makes us feel nervous, scared or small around them.

So often we make assumptions about people that are simply untrue. We assume they're 'above us' or better than us in some way. We assume they're looking down on us or think we're less than they are. And we carry all those assumptions into our interactions with them.

Other times we put people up on a pedestal and idolise them for the power, wealth, fame or success they have achieved. We relate to them as being better than us, more God-like, less human. But in reality, regardless of how rich or famous or powerful or wise anyone is, they're no more 'human' than you. In fact, if you have the opportunity to get to know them, you'll discover they're a lot more like you (that is, fallible and vulnerable) than you think.

**STAND TALL IN YOUR OWN WORTH.
COWER TO NO-ONE.**

Sure there are many people who have accomplished things you haven't. They may hold power that you don't. They may have achieved mastery that you haven't. They may have built a mega-business that you haven't. They may have a million Twitter followers you don't. But they're no better or more worthy than you. So, if you are going to be around people who give rise to your feelings of intimidation, be sure to walk tall in your own value. Cower to no-one but hold yourself as the talented, capable and big-hearted person everyone would want to get to know.

And if, occasionally, you encounter someone who doesn't treat you as worthy, who talks down to you, seeks to coerce you or dismisses you outright, don't take it personally. They're clearly preoccupied with propping up their own ego. Their behaviour doesn't say anything about you; it speaks volumes about them. After all, truly secure and successful people have no need to put others down to lift themselves up. Their behaviour doesn't say anything about you; it speaks volumes about them.

GIVE NO-ONE PERMISSION TO MAKE YOU FEEL SMALL.

You get back from others what you project out. When you expect people to like you and regard you as someone worth knowing, most people will do just that. When you expect people to think you're inconsequential, dull or worthless, you'll likely find they don't respond so positively.

Never let your fear of feeling intimidated or having others not respond to you as you'd like keep you from reaching out to connect with people, to speak assertively and to act confidently. Who knows, maybe you're just the person they need to meet. Maybe they'll find *you* intimidating (it happens!). And perhaps, by owning your power and parking your doubts at the door, you'll forge a rewarding new relationship that opens doors to opportunities you could never have imagined. You'll be amazed by the possibilities that open up when you hold yourself in your power.

Train the brave

What you tell yourself about others, and about yourself, will either lift you up or tear you down; grow your power and influence, or diminish it. So whenever you're with people who may intimidate you, drop all those stories that diminish you. Instead, stand tall and engage with them as you would with any human being, no better or more worthy than you. Then expect good things to follow. Odds are they will, the first being your realisation that you never needed to feel intimidated in the first place.

CHAPTER 27
Don't hide behind humility

Growing up on a farm with six brothers and sisters it was drummed into me from an early age that humility is a virtue, and boasting ... well ... not so much. We were told that if we worked hard and did a good job we'd be recognised for our effort and rewarded accordingly.

For the most part, it was good advice. However, in today's hyper-competitive world, where few people have jobs for life and managers come and go as though through a revolving door, if your plan to get ahead relies on the assumption that hard work is all it takes, you may find yourself being left behind as people no more talented or hardworking than you (and possibly less so!) land the opportunities you anticipated being laid at your own humble hard-working feet. That's not to say hard work isn't important or that humility is no longer a virtue. But too much 'quiet achieving' can leave you languishing. Which is neither good for you nor for those your talents could serve!

Let me be clear though (before you start branding me a braggart!). There's a distinct difference between tooting one's horn to stroke a needy ego and sharing *relevant* information about yourself with the *right* people; that is, people who can help to open the doors for you to thrive and contribute more in your work and life. People who sing their own praises to anyone in earshot are, plain and simple, painful.

THE MORE PEOPLE WHO KNOW WHAT YOU WANT, THE MORE WHO CAN HELP YOU ACHIEVE IT.

I once heard that more than two-thirds of the press releases from General Douglas MacArthur's command during World War II referenced only himself. Of course, that may seem a bit egotistical, but it also highlights the reality that if you don't take responsibility for letting people know what you've done and what you'd like to do, no-one else will.

The old adage, 'It's not what you know, but who you know' no longer holds true. Nowadays, it's not what you know, nor who you know. It's *who knows what you know*! Self-promotion may send a shiver up your spine, but it's really about strategically building your 'personal brand' to ensure that those who can help you achieve what you really want know who you are and what you're up to. Failing to advocate for yourself doesn't serve anyone. Least of all you.

FOCUS ON THE VALUE YOU WANT TO GIVE, NOT WHAT YOU HOPE TO GET.

Perhaps your struggle with blowing your own horn is because you've always viewed it through the lens of what you can get from others. So begin by viewing self-promotion as what it is you'd like to give: about the value that you want to contribute. Reframing from what you can get to what you can give shifts the space you're coming from and how people will perceive you and what you're saying. Sure, you have ambitions you'd like to realise, but bigger than that, you have potential you want to fulfil, talents you want to use and a genuine desire to make a more meaningful contribution that can help others be more successful, not just yourself.

BE PASSIONATE ABOUT WHAT YOU DO.

Anita Roddick, founder of The Body Shop once said, 'To succeed you have to believe in something with such a passion that it becomes a reality'. Likewise, if you want others to support and believe in you, then they need to sense your passion for what you do. You don't have to look very far to find people who lack passion and enthusiasm. So you set yourself apart when you exude it. People notice. They pay attention. They're drawn to it.

By enthusiastically sharing examples of what you've done in the past, what you're working on now and ideas you have for the future, you can convey your value without being a walking (and wearisome) advertorial for You Inc. Of course, just as it's arduous to have to feign interest in your neighbour's photos from their holiday, if people don't have some interest in what you'd love to share, spare them.

DON'T HIDE BEHIND FALSE MODESTY. RISK DISAPPROVAL.

Of course, whenever you put yourself 'out there' and promote yourself (or do pretty much anything that attracts attention!), you run the risk of garnering disapproval or criticism. So be it. Those who criticise are generally saying much more about themselves (their insecurity, envy, misguided humility and fear of being left behind) than they are about you. Letting fear of disapproval determine what you say or do is a sure-fire way never to achieve the success you want. To quote Aristotle: 'To avoid criticism say nothing, do nothing, be nothing'.

Modesty can often just be another form of pride — another way of protecting yourself from judgement and disapproval.

So enough with hiding behind a veil of false modesty! You have value to bring, talent to share and potential to fulfil. It's not just your responsibility to make sure the people who can help you reach your potential know how committed you are to doing so — it's your obligation.

Train the brave

Consider where your fear of appearing boastful is keeping you from letting people know what you've done and what you'd like to do in the future. Then look for opportunities to advocate for yourself to people who can help you make a bigger mark in the world. It's not conceited; it's an act of public service!

CHAPTER 28
Risk more rejections

As I neared the end of writing my first book, *Find Your Courage,* I decided it was time to see if I could find a publisher. I did some research online and put together my 'query letter', which I sent to a long list of publishing houses. In the months that followed, I received dozens of rejection letters and emails. As I opened and read each one it was disheartening. I believed I'd written a book that would be helpful to a lot of people who felt stuck in their lives and yet no publisher was willing to back it. But as discouraging as it was, I kept sending out more letters, all the while plugging along with finishing my book, speaking publicly and writing my monthly newsletter. It wasn't easy, but I hung in there and I'm so glad I did. Because one day, about six months into my rejection marathon, I opened my inbox to find an email from a major publisher who wanted to buy the international rights to my book. I will never forget how thrilled I felt in that moment. *Find Your Courage* was going global!

Of course, most of us barely got through kindergarten without experiencing rejection. But whether you were the only child in your grade-5 class not invited to the birthday party of the year, whether you were passed over for a prized promotion or whether you had the love of your life tell you that you weren't theirs, you've no doubt felt the sting of rejection.

There's no doubt about it, rejection can be very painful and feel intensely personal. But while it's hard not to feel its sting, it's vital not to let your fear of it keep you from risking it.

REJECTION IS NOT ABOUT YOU. WHAT YOU MAKE IT MEAN IS.

You can have the ripest and most delicious strawberry ever grown, but there will still be someone who hates strawberries. The value of my book didn't change after a publisher picked it up. What changed was that someone recognised its value! The truth is, a rejection says far more about the person rejecting — their values, their perceptions, their priorities and indeed their biases, insecurities and fears — than it does about the person who has been rejected. Maybe they weren't up for the relationship or commitment. Maybe they thought you were over-qualified and would quickly get bored. Maybe the timing was off. They made that decision based on their subjective assessment — one shaped by their concerns, values, assumptions, opinions and unconscious biases. The rejection means no more, or less, than that. The rest is pure conjecture.

The part of rejection that relates to you is about the spin you put on it; that is, the story you tell yourself about why you were rejected and the subsequent actions you take. If you interpret a rejection as proof that you are unemployable or unlovable or doomed to never achieve what you want, you'll find it tough going to do whatever is needed to achieve the result you want. Rather than chastise yourself or wallow in self-pity, make the most of the opportunity to learn and grow, and set yourself up for more success in the future. As poet and author Sylvia Plath once wrote, 'I love my rejection slips. They show me I try'.

DON'T WASTE YOUR REJECTIONS; LEARN AND GROW FROM THEM.

Talk to any truly successful person and they'll tell you they'd never have got to where they are had they not been willing to risk rejection. Again and again and again. They'll also tell you that they provided invaluable opportunities to gain useful feedback, to polish their offer and fine-tune how they presented it and themselves. If you didn't get the second interview, find out what they wanted in their ideal candidate. If you were passed over for that promotion, ask what it is you need to strengthen to get it next time. Opportunities go to those who stay proactive even when they aren't getting the results they want. The more often you're willing to put yourself on the line, the sooner you'll get over it.

THE MORE YOU PUT YOURSELF 'OUT THERE', THE SOONER YOU'LL LAND WHAT YOU WANT.

Obviously, if you're reading this now you know that I've since been 'lucky' (three times!) in having a book published. Which is what tends to happen when we're willing to risk rejection: we strike it lucky! But not really. Because it's not luck; it's arithmetic. The more you put yourself out there, the greater are your odds of getting 'lucky' and creating amazing opportunities, building new and rich relationships and achieving what truly excites you.

As my dad always says, 'You've got to be in it to win it'. By refusing to get sucked into negative comparisons, self-rebuke and self-pity you can rise above your 'rejections' and do the very things you need to do to bump yourself up to the top of the list.

REJECTION NEVER HURTS FOR AS LONG AS REGRET.

Too often we spend our lives avoiding any possibility of rejection. Our fear of being judged as unworthy keeps us from putting ourselves 'out there'. But just imagine the possibilities that would open up for you if you were willing to risk rejection and embrace the belief that doing so was crucial to achieving what you truly wanted in your work, relationships and life.

So stop making rejection mean anything about how worthy you are or the value you bring. Dare to risk being rejected more often — not to injure your pride, but to expand your possibilities. Isn't that worth the occasional sting? To quote Bear Grylls: 'If you risk nothing, you gain nothing'.

Train the brave

If you were not going to let your fear of rejection hold you back, where would you put yourself 'out there' and risk rejection for the sake of something bigger?

CHAPTER 29

Be decisive amid uncertainty

For more than 20 years, my husband Andrew has worked for an international company that has moved him into many different roles in different places around the world. Professionally, it's provided him with a diverse array of challenging and rewarding experiences. Personally, it's afforded our family with some wonderful experiences. However, I'd be lying if I said it'd been one long, globe-trotting cakewalk as we made our way from one exciting adventure to another.

Not knowing where we might be living next, or when we would next have to pack up our home, farewell our friends, uproot from schools, leave our community and build a new one in an unfamiliar city or country hasn't been without its challenges or anxiety. I've certainly had my fair share of 'special moments' as I've juggled (and dropped) the balls of raising children and pursuing my own professional aspirations, all while relocating homes and hemispheres. Of course, we've always had the choice to pull the pin and say 'Enough!', but we've ultimately decided that the benefits — individually and collectively — have outweighed the costs.

While my situation is unique, it's held two valuable lessons. The first is how important it is to accept uncertainty as a mainstay of life. The second is how much needless and paralysing anxiety we can create for ourselves when we don't.

LIFE REWARDS ACTION, NOT INDECISION.

Let's face it, we all live with uncertainty — today more than ever. Whether you've been in the same job or home your entire life or had the standard seven careers (which is the new norm), none of us can look into the future and know for sure what it holds. The world we live in today is in a rapid state of change with no slow-down in sight. Markets are changing. Consumer habits are changing. The global economy is changing. The top 10 jobs today didn't exist 10 years ago. Nor did a dozen new countries. Nor did Twitter or, for that matter, the ability to bring down a regime through social media. Despite all the work done to predict the future, no-one can ever know what it holds.

And don't I know! Early in our marriage, Andrew and I spent inordinate amounts of time trying to predict *what* his next role might be, *where* it might be and *how* we'd manage my career, our children and the logistics around it (a task that has become increasingly complex as our children have grown older). Yet despite what we felt was excellent analysis, time and time again our predictions turned out utterly wrong. It took us a few years of massive speculative failures to realise that there were far too many variables beyond our knowledge and control at play and that trying to predict the future was an exercise in futility.

SOME PEOPLE LIVE THEIR LIVES ON HOLD WAITING TO MAKE THE PERFECT DECISION.

We all want to make decisions today based on a tomorrow we can predict with certainty. It's human nature. But if you're waiting for certainty before you commit to a plan of action, you can spend your life on hold. It's why wherever I've lived, including where I live now, I've just lived as though I'm here forever. If I had held back on forging ahead in my career, establishing friendships or building networks because I didn't know how long I'd be somewhere I'd have missed out on meeting some phenomenal people, and enjoying some amazing experiences and opportunities.

Of course, I've also made a few decisions that — had I known what would lay ahead — I'd have made differently. But that's life for all of us. Life's unpredictability makes decision-making harder. But to succeed in life you have to embrace uncertainty as part and parcel of life and be willing to just take action, to live decisively, despite it. As Lee Iacocca, former president of Ford and Chrysler, once said, 'The one word that makes a good manager — decisiveness'. The best way to build decisiveness is to start where you are with the next decision you face.

THE MOST DANGEROUS DECISION IS NOT TO MAKE ONE.

Of course, for many people, even without much uncertainty, making decisions can be stressful. Should you stay in your job or look for a new one? Buy a house or keep renting? Sell your house or sit on it longer? Continue in your secure salaried job or go out on your own? Stay in your relationship or leave it? Send your kids to public school or private? Move them to a new school or keep them where they are? Move Dad into a nursing home or hire extra home care? The stress we create for ourselves by trying to make the right choice — the 'perfect' choice — only amplifies our decision anxiety.

We're wired to want to feel in control of the future as it unfolds ahead of us. You wouldn't be human if you didn't have a part of you that wanted to know what your life would look like one, five or ten years from now. This is why making decisions amid uncertainty is an act of courage. It demands having faith in yourself that however your future unfolds, you'll handle it, thereby easing your fear of the unknown and inviting you to be more proactive in shaping it.

BETTER TO MAKE A WRONG DECISION NOW THAN TO BE PARALYSED BY INDECISION.

Rather than trying to predict the future, or — even more futile — worrying how you'll handle it if it doesn't unfold to plan, you're far better off focusing on making the best decisions you can right now, with what you know now. If the future doesn't unfold as predicted, you can adjust accordingly. But making no decision for fear of making a wrong one is usually far more risky than just making a call. As Jewish philosopher Maimonides wrote in the eleventh century, 'The risk of a wrong decision is preferable to the terror of indecision'.

It's a general rule in psychology that for people to make the decision to change something it has to hurt more now than it hurts to change it. But what if right now you aren't hurting very much, with no pressing 'pain point'? Then think about the pain you might feel down the track if you stick with the status quo, decide nothing and do nothing. What pain might you feel then? What pain might your unwillingness to make a decision cause those around you? It may be more than you want to acknowledge.

INACTION DOESN'T MAKE YOU MORE SECURE; IT MAKES YOU LESS SO.

Allowing your fear of the unknown to occupy the driver's seat won't set you up to handle whatever your future brings. It may sound counterintuitive, but avoiding change because the future is uncertain doesn't make you more secure; it makes you less so. Not taking action because it invites greater uncertainty into your life is never a good reason not to take it. In fact, it's a pretty lousy one. Sure, there's no guarantee that your best decision today will result in the outcomes you want. But trying to avoid uncertainty by sticking with the status quo can leave you living permanently on hold. From my perspective, that's a pretty crummy way to live.

No-one knows exactly what the world will look like 10 years from now. But what is certain is that those who embrace uncertainty as part and parcel of life will be those best positioned to seize the opportunities our uncertain future will inevitably present. I promise.

Train the brave

Putting off making a decision often feels safe in the present moment, but always comes with an opportunity cost. Where do you need to 'bite the bullet' and just make a decision despite your uncertainty?

CHAPTER 30
Unlearn to relearn

Carton by carton, I unwrapped possessions I'd not seen for many years. Not since we'd moved from Australia to the United States more than a decade earlier and, truth be told, I couldn't for the life of me remember what we'd left behind in storage. Then again, I had a five-week-old baby and two toddlers at the time, so my memory of that entire period was shrouded in a sleep-deprived haze. So I took to each cardboard carton with a box cutter. I felt like I was opening up a long lost Egyptian tomb ... what forgotten treasures might I discover inside?

As luck would have it, not many.

What emerged from copious amounts of wrapping paper was not so much treasure but worthless relics from a distant past. Old plant tubs, complete with dried prehistoric snails (honestly, what was I thinking?). Scratched photo frames. An electric fry pan. And — the highlight — a brick-sized medieval cordless phone. Ironically enough, my youngest child Matthew thought it was pretty cool. 'You could get money selling this one!' he said enthusiastically. I doubted that very much.

Unpacking those boxes brought home to me how much can change in a decade. Not just phones, but simply the procession of life. When I turned on the television, I was introduced to 'famous' celebrities I'd never laid eyes on. When I got in my car, I discovered new tunnels I didn't know existed. It felt a bit like I was living inside an Austin Powers movie.

Of course, over the prior 10 years there had been people who had made their fortune and a lot who had lost it. Companies had folded and empires had been built. Technology created and technology laid to rest. Needless to say, a lot can change in 10 years. Which begs the question, how must we change in order to thrive in the world we'll be inhabiting 10 years from now?

A CURIOUS MIND WILL TAKE YOU FURTHER THAN A CLEVER ONE.

Philosopher Eric Hoffer once wrote that it is unlearners who will inherit the future: 'The learned usually find themselves equipped to live in a world that no longer exists'. The concept of 'unlearning' seems a bit foreign to most of us. After all, you're constantly bombarded with new knowledge you feel compelled to learn, not to unlearn. But that's precisely the point. Unless you're willing to let go some of the knowledge that's helped get you to where you are today, you'll limit your capacity to learn the new knowledge required to take you to where you want to go in the future.

Unlearning is a bit like pulling out the old plants and weeds from your garden so that others can blossom. It requires trading answers for questions; cleverness for curiosity; certainty for wonder. In the space of unlearning what you *think* you know you create the possibility of learning what you *need* to know. Needless to say, trading your answers for questions requires bravery because it demands exposing yourself as being less knowledgeable — less clever — than you like to think. As Albert Einstein once wrote, 'The important thing is not to stop questioning. Curiosity has its own reason for existing'.

THE FUTURE BELONGS TO THOSE WHO PREPARE FOR IT TODAY.

While I don't know what you need to unlearn, I'd hazard a guess that you, like me, are walking through each day with knowledge, beliefs and answers that are insufficient to thrive in the world of tomorrow. For instance, the way you used to manage your career, your diary, your money and your communication 10 years ago will most certainly not be the best way to manage it 10 years from now. On a societal level, the way we educated our children, handled immigration, tackled terrorism or provided social welfare in the past will not set us up to achieve optimal outcomes in the future. To quote Malcom X, 'Tomorrow belongs only to the people who prepare for it today'.

Sometimes success can lull us into complacency, along with a false sense of confidence in our approach and ourselves. In his book *What Got You Here Won't Get You There,* Marshall Goldsmith, a coaching colleague, wrote that, 'One of the greatest mistakes of successful people is the assumption, "I behave this way, and I achieve results. Therefore, I must be achieving results because I behave this way".' Sure, what you did in the past may be partly attributed to your success today, but don't count on it cutting the grade in the future.

You won't get ahead in today's ever-changing world only by continuing to do what you've always done, just better and better. Rather, you'll get ahead by proactively engaging in the world around you, learning new skills, new technology, new processes and new approaches and by being open to the new opportunities change always holds. To quote Bill Clinton, 'The price of doing the same old thing is far higher than the price of change'.

Feminist Gloria Steinem once said, 'The first problem for all of us, men and women, is not to learn, but to unlearn'. While it's entirely normal to hold tight to what we've learned so far and resist the unknown and untested, thriving in our accelerated world requires having the courage to embrace the new, let go the familiar and unlearn the learned. The cost of not doing so is being left behind as the opportunities change. You have too much to offer, and too much to lose, to let that happen.

Train the brave

There's an old saying that you can't move forward in old carriages. Likewise, the knowledge, processes and assumptions that got you to where you are today will be insufficient to get you to where you want to go 10 years from now. So, as you look forward to the future, what must you adapt to, what must you learn, what must you unlearn and what must you let go?

CHAPTER 31
Seek expert advice, but apply it sparingly

Career advice. Business advice. Financial advice. Parenting advice. Relationship advice. Fashion advice. Legal advice. Marketing advice. Dieting advice.

I'm sure you've been given plenty of advice over the years. Some of it you may have even paid for. No doubt there have been times when you've taken someone's advice: followed their formula, bought their solutions, administered their treatments and changed your strategy. I certainly have. Like the time I was told that yellow was my colour.

'Yellow is definitely your colour,' pronounced the colour 'expert' to me as I tried on a yellow blazer as part of her multi-step system to identify my colours. I bought the jacket. A yellow shirt too. I wore the jacket once and the shirt twice. Every time thereafter I'd put them on and then promptly hang them back up. I just don't like how I look in yellow. I ended up giving both to my gorgeous Italian friend Maria. Yellow suited her!

NO ENEMY IS WORSE THAN BAD ADVICE.

I've had enough misfires over the years to know that while expert advice can be valuable, no expert can ever know for sure what's right for you. More so, that if someone's expert opinion just doesn't sit well with you, you should park it and move on. Imagine what the world would have missed out on had the Beatles not done that after being told they had the wrong sound and that guitar music was on the way out by a leading record company executive in 1962.

Of course, it takes courage to discard the advice of someone regarded as an expert. Even more if they've come to you with a strong personal recommendation. Likewise, it's tempting to want to hand authority over to the 'internationally renowned', 'highly acclaimed', 'guru', 'adviser to the stars' to 'fix' your problem. I've met many people who go from one advice guru to another looking for the magical 10-step formula to eternal youth, making a quick million (with no risk!), attracting the perfect (rich and extremely good looking) soul mate, or whatever it is they're yearning for. Too many!

NEVER HAND ANYONE BLANKET AUTHORITY TO DECIDE WHAT'S RIGHT FOR YOU.

I once had a woman I'd never met before approach me after speaking at a large event to ask, without any preamble, 'Should I divorce my husband?' The fact that I knew nothing about her, her husband or her marriage was obviously irrelevant to her. What disturbed me was how ready she was to trust my snap judgement on such an important decision. I may have been married for more than 20 years, but I'm not a marriage expert. And even if I were, and I'd known her for years, it would still have been unwise to give me so much authority. Yet the fact that she did reflects how quick some people can be to hand over the reins of their ambitions, pension fund, business, careers, relationships, wardrobes, health, bodies and beliefs to people they deem know more about what's right for them than they do.

CONSULT YOUR OWN INNER SAGE. IT KNOWS BETTER THAN ANYONE WHAT'S RIGHT FOR YOU.

Of course, there are many experts whose wisdom and insights can help us build our businesses, nurture our relationships, pursue our goals and live our lives more successfully. But as wise, credentialed and experienced as some people may be in their field of expertise, no-one can ever know what's right for you. Just because their prescription for success worked for them or others, doesn't mean it will work for you or even that it's right for you!

I told the woman that I really couldn't give her any advice about ending her marriage: that this was a decision she alone had to make. I encouraged her to journal about it, to pray on it and to see a counsellor with her husband. I'm not sure whether she ever did. There was something about her eagerness for me to decide the fate of her marriage that made me wonder whether she would rather find someone else (another 'expert') to take responsibility for her happiness than own it herself. And therein lay what was likely eating at her marriage to begin with: a lack of belief in her own judgement and worthiness. The bigger lesson: you and *only you* must take responsibility for the choices you make; and you, and only you, can know which ones are right.

So whatever challenges or opportunities you're facing right now, be proactive in seeking advice from people who may have insight and experience that you don't. But don't give them blanket authority to rewrite your aspirations, rebrand your business or redesign your life. Rather, listen to what they say, but consult your own inner sage before moving on. It knows more than anyone what's best for you. That's my expert advice anyway! Take what resonates; ditch what doesn't.

Train the brave

Never let the noise of other opinions drown out your own. Where have you given too much authority to experts only to look back and realise that they didn't have a monopoly on wisdom? Where do you need to reclaim some of the authority you've previously given away, and take more ownership for navigating your own best path forward? After all, no-one knows what you have to bring to the world more than you do, and no-one cares more about your success.

CHAPTER 32

Lift others as you climb

Over the years I've learned that not every opportunity or client is the right one for me, and nor am I the best person for them. So I've built a broad referral network to refer people on to whenever I assess that they'd be a better fit or simply find more value elsewhere. Ironically enough, the more I've referred people on to others the more work has flowed back to me and the more enjoyment I've had from the opportunities, people and organisations I have engaged with.

Of course, there are many people who have a similar mindset. People who are secure in their value and unthreatened by the value, talent and strengths of others. However, I've also encountered many who haven't shared my mindset. Likely because they feel that helping someone else succeed will lower the odds that they will succeed too — as though there's only so much opportunity to go around. The fear that feeds this scarcity mindset drives people to see every situation as 'win–lose'. That is, if I help you get something, then I'll have to lose something. It can keep people from sharing a great resource, sending on a referral or making an introduction that could help someone else move forward. And while people with a win–lose mentality can always find ample reasons to justify it, the truth is that when you lift others, you lift yourself. As Napolean Hill wrote, 'You can succeed best and quickest by helping others to succeed'.

BEING GENEROUS CONFRONTS OUR FEAR OF MISSING OUT.

While operating from an abundance mindset nurtures our innate desire to be helpful — to practise generosity with our money, words, connections, resources or time — it also confronts our fear of missing out. Which is why, in a world that's constantly warning us about the imminent shortage of resources, generosity is an act of courage. It's courageous because it means having faith that when you give more away, you'll not be left with less and that when you help someone else get ahead, you won't be left behind. Where the abundance mindset flows from faith, the scarcity mindset stems from fear.

Choosing to go out of your way to help others succeed, including those some might consider your competitors, requires putting aside your FOMO — Fear Of Missing Out — and dialling up your faith in the goodness of others and the good-old law of karma. Our every action is a force of energy that returns to us in kind so when we choose to act in ways that help others, we reap the fruit of our giving. What goes around, comes around. St Francis Assisi said it best of all: 'It is in giving that you receive'.

Don't let your fear of missing out on an opportunity or greater success keep you from enabling more of both for others. When you're living in alignment with your deepest values and highest purpose, you'll find that there's an abundance of opportunity for you and those you consider your competitors. When you lift others, you lift yourself.

WHEN WE LIFT OTHERS, WE LIFT OURSELVES, EVEN IF THEY DON'T SAY THANK YOU.

Sometimes giving a few words of encouragement to someone who's been doing it tough can make all the difference between them throwing in the towel and hanging in there another day, during which a light appears in what has been a long, dark tunnel. Sometimes taking a few minutes of your time to make an introduction or share some advice can open a new door that puts someone on an entirely new trajectory in their work or life.

The first time I heard about coaching was when a guy I barely knew called me up out of the blue to say he'd heard about this new field of coaching. There was nothing in it for him, but he wanted to let me know about it. 'It just sounded like something that would be a good fit for you,' he said and encouraged me to check it out. I did. It set me on a new path, which has led me to typing these words you're reading right now.

HAVE FAITH. PAY IT FORWARD.

Of course, people don't always return a kindness with a kindness or a favour with a favour. But that doesn't mean you should only be generous to those who you know will return it to you. Be the change you want to see in others and help them anyway. Because over the years, the law of reciprocity will ultimately come into play as others extend support to you from places you never considered.

BE GENEROUS WITH ENCOURAGEMENT. MOST PEOPLE ARE HUNGRY FOR IT.

To share a Buddhist saying, 'If you light a lamp for somebody, it will also brighten your path'.

So how about you? Where can you give a 'lift up' to someone today, whether it's writing a recommendation on LinkedIn, offering some mentoring, information about a course or a conference you think they'd enjoy, an invitation to dinner or an introduction to someone you sense they'd love to know? Whatever resistance you may feel in going out of your way, take a big, brave breath and release it. The best part of you, the *biggest* part of you and the *bravest* part of you knows better. Be that positive change you want to see in the world, starting with giving others the support you've sometimes wished for yourself. A rising tide lifts all boats.

Train the brave

Who can you extend a helping hand to today—not because it makes you look good, but simply because it's your outward expression of the inner changes you're making in your life? The extra bonus you get is that, over time, your generosity will come back to you tenfold. Just wait. Just watch. Keep faith.

Part IV
Dig deep

How to be resilient when life doesn't go to plan

CHAPTER 33
Life doesn't happen to you, it happens for you

When Lynika Cruz was 14 years old, her mother left her on the roadside and told her it was time she fended for herself. In her school backpack were a few dollars, a change of clothes, one book and a couple of pieces of fruit.

For the next 12 months Lynika lived on the streets, surviving on her own wits, eating old bread from the back of bakeries and sleeping in trees at night. She was desperate to avoid being discovered as homeless by welfare and put into the foster system. She feared that it would be a replica of the chaotic, violent experience of her own family.

On her fifteenth birthday, Lynika located her mother, who still did not want her back. Shortly after, she found a job. It enabled her to get off the streets and into a small, rented caravan. She then put herself through correspondence school while working, going on to later earn three university degrees and a Doctorate in Humanistic Science.

YOU ARE STRONGER THAN ANYTHING YOU FACE.

When I met Lynika, who was now a grown woman speaking around the world, I was struck by not only her poise, but by what a warm and self-assured woman she was for someone who had come through such a turbulent childhood. I asked her what had helped her to emerge through so much adversity, heartache, rejection and loss with such grace.

'Seven words,' she said. 'I am stronger than what I face.'

Those seven words hold power because they reveal a truth — a truth that we need to remind ourselves of time and time again. So often when we face a situation that seems insurmountable, we become overwhelmed by how we can ever overcome the enormity of what we're confronting. It seems so huge. We feel so small. But no matter how big your hurdles, large your loss or overwhelming your circumstances, within you lie all the resources you ever need to handle it. Sometimes we just don't know how brave we are until being brave is our only choice.

ADVERSITY INTRODUCES US TO OURSELVES.

Mary Tyler Moore once said that you can't be brave if you've only had wonderful things happen to you. Of course, sometimes you have to be braver than you want to be. But it's those times when you felt way out of your league in the courage department that you discovered your own inner Braveheart. Adversity has a potent way of introducing us to ourselves and revealing us to ourselves, and of uncovering deeper aspects of our own humanity and bringing them to the fore. Difficult times introduce us not only to more of who we are right now, but to who we have it within us to become — to the creativity, tenacity, power and determination we didn't know we had. So embrace your adversities not just as trials to go through or suffering to be endured, but as experiences to grow through and lessons to be learned. To quote poet Samuel Johnson, 'Adversity has ever been considered the state in which a man most easily becomes acquainted with himself'.

When you're facing uncertain and turbulent times, it's easy to get lured into worrying about how you'll handle what might happen 10 years from now, one year from now or even one week from now. While some planning ahead is useful, wasting energy fretting about what lies around the bend is not. Rather, focus on what's directly ahead, placing faith in yourself, and in the power that created you, that you're stronger than anything you'll face and you have everything it takes to meet your challenges — however large, however daunting — one day, one hour, one moment at a time. Doing that will make all the difference.

Train the brave

When you trust yourself to handle the challenges life brings your way, it lightens the burden and expands your capacity to face those challenges with greater courage, optimism and resilience. What new ways of dealing with your current challenges open up for you simply by trusting in yourself more deeply?

CHAPTER 34

Refuse to let your circumstances define you

What doesn't kill you makes you stronger.

The fact that these words by German philosopher Friedrich Nietzsche are so famous doesn't make them true. I'm sure you've encountered numerous people who have survived a hardship or heartache and haven't emerged from it stronger and better off, but weaker and worse off and very much a 'victim' to their 'lot in life'. This is why I believe Nietzsche got it wrong: it's not the hardship itself that makes us stronger, but rather how we choose — and yes, *it is a choice* — to respond to it. The good news is that the choice is entirely at your disposal.

My friend Michelle McQuaid, an expert in positive psychology, views the difficult hardships, hurdles and heartaches of our lives as gifts we never asked for and don't want, but something that we may as well make the most of. Approaching your shake-ups, break-ups and wake-ups with this mindset can make all the difference in the world to how well you handle them and how strong you emerge from them. As Greek philosopher Horace wrote, 'Adversity has the effect of eliciting talents, which in prosperous circumstances would have lain dormant'.

Of course, it's all too easy to get pulled into our own little pity party when life doesn't go to plan. It's why many do. But by doing so you relinquish your power, surrender your freedom and confine your ability to shape, and improve, your future. Rising above the circumstances you find yourself in begins with acceptance that life will often not go to plan and that every time it doesn't, you have a choice: to be defined by your circumstances, or to be bigger than them. Consciously choosing the latter gives you access to a vast reservoir of grit and ingenuity that may otherwise have lain dormant.

YOU CAN'T ALWAYS CHOOSE YOUR CIRCUMSTANCES BUT YOU CAN ALWAYS CHOOSE YOUR RESPONSE TO THEM. THEREIN LIES YOUR POWER.

I don't know what challenges you are facing right now. What troubles you have in your family. What pressures you have in your work. What strain you have on your finances. What aches you have in your heart. But I know that every experience you've had has brought you to where you are today and that right now you're exactly where you're supposed to be, armed with everything you need within you to respond more constructively, calmly and courageously. And while accidents do happen, you reading this now isn't one.

Too often we buy into the misguided belief that it's our circumstances that determine our happiness, and that our success is dependent on good luck, good genes or good fortune. Taking ownership of your life is an act of courage because it requires letting go excuses, justifications and blame and taking full and complete responsibility for your day-by-day, moment-by-moment experience. No matter what.

YOU – AND ONLY YOU – ARE RESPONSIBLE FOR YOUR HAPPINESS.

You and *only you* are responsible for your happiness. Don't abdicate responsibility for others to make you happy. Don't blame others when you're not. Don't sit around waiting for someone to make things better. Don't wait for others to help you do it. Just get up from where you are now and get on with doing whatever you can see needs to be done *right* now. Giving your best today, even if it feels like it's not enough, will help you face tomorrow better still.

Happiness in life doesn't depend on everything going your way. It doesn't depend on things working out well for you at every turn. It doesn't depend on people treating you nicely and acting honestly. It doesn't even depend on you enjoying human rights, good health or prosperity. It's the fruit of taking responsibility for what you do when times are good — 'working hard at work worth doing' — and when times are tough. When you give your best to making things better — no matter how bad they are — you'll find the universe will conspire with you to make it so. It just needs to see that you're first willing to do your part. As Sophocles wrote two thousand years ago, 'Heaven never helps the man who will not act'.

People who are truly successful in life are never victim to their circumstances; they're always bigger than them. So whatever is not as you'd like it right now, don't make excuses for why it is as it is, and why you can't do anything about it. Rather, get up from your seat, roll up your sleeves and do what you can to make things better. If opportunity doesn't knock, build a door. If people let you down, pick yourself up. If plans fall apart, make new ones. However bleak it may seem or weak you may feel, there are always things you can do to make things better!

Train the brave

Resilient. Strong. Courageous. Bold. Determined. Optimistic. Tenacious. Accepting. Persistent. Enthusiastic. Committed. Passionate. Purposeful. Powerful. Resourceful. Faithful. Light hearted. Self-reliant. Compassionate. Disciplined. Generous. Proactive. Assertive. Trusting. Confident.

Choose three words that you want to define who you will be in the face of the challenges you face today. Then, bring to mind a problem you're facing and ask yourself, what would I do right now if I were being really [insert your word]? Whatever answer comes to mind first, act on it. If opportunity doesn't knock, build a door. If people let you down, pick yourself up. If plans fall apart, make new ones. This holds the power to transform your problem into an opportunity.

CHAPTER 35

Nurture resilience daily; courage calls for it

When I was nearly five months pregnant with my first child I found myself with a sawn-off shotgun at my forehead in an armed robbery while living in Port Moresby in Papua New Guinea. While I knew that PNG was a violent country, it had never occurred to me that I might one day experience its lawlessness so directly. Ten days later I learned that my unborn baby had died.

The two events, back to back, turned my world on its axis. Up until then, despite the challenges I'd faced, I'd lived by the assumption that bad things such as being caught in a robbery or losing an unborn baby happened to other people. In the months that followed I was forced to dig deep as two more miscarriages further challenged my faith and knocked at my confidence.

However, as people extended sympathy to me, I can remember thinking to myself that I wouldn't allow myself to be defined as a victim. Yes, I'd had a tough time, but I didn't want it to define me. I worked hard to keep my head in the right space. I swam daily; wrote in my journal daily (sometimes twice a day); prayed frequently; ran regularly; spent a lot of time with my closest friends; and read a lot of books to help me process my experience and face my future with optimism.

While some days I did better than others, I was instinctively drawn to the people and activities that would help to build my resilience. Following my instincts enabled me to emerge from that period stronger, wiser and far more resilient than I'd gone into it.

RESILIENCE IS INDISPENSABLE TO LIVING BRAVELY.

Resilience is defined by our ability to bounce back from setbacks, adapt to change, handle pressure and cope with life when it doesn't go to plan. Needless to say, it's indispensable for living bravely. It not only helps us to cope better with life's unexpected heartaches and hurdles, but it boosts our confidence to pursue bigger and more meaningful goals and endeavours.

RESILIENCE ISN'T WHAT YOU HAVE; IT'S WHAT YOU DO.

There's no doubt that we each arrive into the world with our own distinct personality. Some people have thicker skin. Some a higher tolerance for pressure. Others are more adaptable to change and eager for adventure. But while we have our own type of innate resilience, every one of us can strengthen it. That's because resilience (like courage) is not a fixed attribute — it's not something you've either got or not. In fact, new research into neural plasticity (your brain's ability to change itself) has proven that everyone — including the most sensitive and timid — can strengthen their ability to handle setbacks more positively, adapt to change more flexibly and cope with pressure more calmly.

DAILY 'RESILIENCE-BUILDING' HABITS SOW THE SEEDS FOR LASTING RESULTS.

The small, habitual things you do each day have a large impact on your ability to succeed in the bigger game of life. While they're often outside your conscious awareness, your daily habits can profoundly impact your ability to stay focused, calm and confident when pressures mount and plans fall apart. While it may sound unfair to some, our success in life lies in direct proportion to what's left when our unhealthy habits of thought and behaviour are subtracted from our good ones!

A car that gets taken in for regular tune-ups goes further on less petrol and breaks down less often. Likewise, if you're constantly driving yourself at full speed, or carrying a particularly heavy load with little or no time out to 'tune-up', you'll eventually burn out. Studies show that the intensity of your job or demands of your life aren't what lead to burnout. It's the duration of time you go without being able to stop, rest and recover.

Regularly taking time to disengage enables you to re-engage with greater passion, focus and effectiveness. And if you're telling yourself you're too busy to take one hour to renew and recharge, it's a sure sign you need to take two.

MAKE TIME TO DO WHATEVER FUELS YOUR STRENGTH – BODY, MIND AND SPIRIT

It's a well-worn saying that nothing worthwhile is accomplished in our comfort zone. But that's not quite true. If you're constantly living and working outside your comfort zone, it's important to retreat to it to do whatever replenishes your reserves and refuels your bravery. The nature of my own work means that sometimes a series of large presentations and deadlines fall close together. The pressure of juggling many balls, managing commitments and meeting expectations can take a toll. When it does, I can feel my body growing tense and my sleep patchy. As my kids and husband will tell you, I'm never at my best on a lack of sleep! So whenever I have a lot on my plate, I'm extra intentional about fitting in my morning run or writing in my journal (I've kept one since I was 11) or, schedule permitting, taking a quick nap. Likewise, when you've got a lot on your plate, the best thing you can do for yourself is to declare yourself a guilt-free zone — even for a few minutes — to do whatever helps you to return to being your 'best self'. For example:

» stop moving and sit still so you can hear what your intuition is telling you

» spend time with people who make you laugh, lift you up or let you cry (and avoid those who don't!)

» head outdoors to commune with nature

» move your body, relax your body, stretch your body

» listen to music or play it

» write in your journal or read something that lifts you

» play with your kids, walk your dog, or take a nap

Abraham Lincoln once said, 'If I had eight hours to chop down a tree, I'd spend six sharpening my axe'. The sharper your axe, the more resilient, courageous and effective you'll be in every domain of your life. You're never too busy to take time to sharpen your axe. You're too busy *not* to. It's not just an act of self-service, it's an act of public service! So make a commitment to invest time more regularly in doing whatever helps you to put your best (and bravest) foot forward every day, particularly when it's outside your comfort zone. It's not just helpful for living well, it's essential.

Train the brave

Confucius wrote, 'Our natures are alike. It's our habits that separate us'. Accordingly, it's the seemingly small things you do on a regular basis to bolster your resilience that refuel your courage to create the big results that everyone wants. Take a moment to consider what you could start doing differently in the following areas:

» *Physically.* What could you start doing each day or week to help you feel healthier and stronger, with the stamina and energy you need to do what you want?

» *Mentally.* What could you start doing to help you stay focused on your highest priorities and avoid getting caught up with distractions?

» *Emotionally.* What activities could you incorporate into each day to help you manage anxiety and other potentially destructive emotions, enabling you to face each day with greater self-confidence, humour and optimism?

» *Spiritually.* What rituals could you cultivate to help you reconnect and realign more often with your highest purpose in life?

CHAPTER 36
Asking for help reveals strength, not weakness

Mona and I became friends in 2002, about eight months after I had moved to the United States from Australia. We each had three young children and before too long we were both expecting a fourth. While we were both busy, Mona always gave me a reality check, recalibrating what it meant to be busy. While I was studying psychology part-time, she was a vice president at the American Heart Association. Needless to say, she was my version of a Superwoman (and still is!).

Six years after we met, Mona noticed a sore on her breast. She checked it with doctors but a full six months passed until she was finally given a diagnosis. Breast cancer ... stage 3 ... highly aggressive. A diagnosis no woman ever wants to hear, yet which too many do. The prognosis was not good. In the months that followed, Mona underwent a potent cocktail of chemotherapy drugs, dual mastectomy, radiation, reconstruction and then a full hysterectomy. The doctors were pleased with her response, but the following year, the cancer was back, now with a stage-4 diagnosis. More surgery, more chemo, more radiation. Only those who have endured it, or witnessed someone who has, can know how debilitating it can be. However less than a year after being given another clean bill of health, Mona collapsed near her home while out for a walk. An MRI found 15 tumors in her brain. More radiation, Gamma Knife surgery, more medicine, more prayers. All the while Mona and her husband tried to create as normal family life as they could for their four children.

As I write this now, it is close to six years since that original diagnosis. While not living in Dallas any more means I don't see as much of Mona as I'd like, I'm incredibly grateful that she is still here and I love reading her faith-filled updates and seeing her whenever I can swing a stop-over in Dallas. Her deep faith, resilience and courage never fail to inspire me.

ASKING FOR HELP PROVIDES PEOPLE A CHANCE TO GIVE THEIR GIFTS.

There are countless lessons I've learned from sharing Mona's journey. One of the most precious is how important it is to reach out and ask for help when life's pressures and problems weigh heavily upon us. As a fiercely independent and immensely capable woman, this was hard for Mona in the beginning. Like so many people (myself included), Mona found it far more comfortable to lend a hand to others, than to receive it. But over time she came to realise that not only could she no longer manage everything on her own, but that not accepting offers to help, and not asking for favours when she needed them, deprived everyone of the gift of friendship that can enrich our lives so deeply.

While talking to her recently Mona shared this with me, 'I distinctly remember God whispering in my heart that it all came from him and there was never a way to pay it back'. That whisper is one we all need to hear at times — not to let our pride keep us from asking for help and opening our hearts to receiving kindness, support, guidance or gifts, even though we may never be able to return them in the same way or the same measure. All we can ever do is to be open to opportunities to extend help to others, in whatever way we see the need, and to let go ever needing for it to be returned or acknowledged.

ASK FOR HELP NOT BECAUSE YOU'RE WEAK BUT BECAUSE YOU WANT TO STAY STRONG.

The African proverb 'It takes a village' holds truth far beyond the challenges of raising children. We all need to feel part of some 'village' to meet the challenges we face in life with the bravery needed to handle them better and emerge better off. Belonging to a community sustains our strength and connectedness bolsters our resilience. As Anne Deveson wrote in *Resilience*, 'Never underestimate the value of friendship in surviving difficult times'. Without it, our innate resilience to weather turbulent times can grow increasingly fragile.

Keeping your problems to yourself isn't brave. Stoic, yes. Brave, no. What's brave is having the courage to share your vulnerability, to expose your struggle, to reveal your humanity and to ask for help when you need it. Not just when you know you can return the favour, but even more so, when you know you can't. The way I see it, God wouldn't have given us friends if we were meant to carry our burdens alone. As the proverb says, 'A burden shared is a burden halved'.

Reaching out to ask for help, and accepting it when offered, is not a sign of weakness; it's a sign of strength. When you put aside your pride and ask for help, not only do you benefit from the support you get, but you give others an opportunity to extend friendship, to practise generosity, to feel valued and to learn it's okay to ask for help themselves. Everyone is better off.

So don't let your fear of appearing weak, fragile, lost or needy keep you from reaching out, from sharing your burden and asking others to help you carry some of it. It's when we lay bare the burdens we carry that we make ourselves available to connect most deeply with those around us and forge the bonds that can help us weather the biggest storms. Together we're far more than the sum of our parts; together we can go further, stand stronger and fly higher than we ever can alone.

Train the brave

Where is fear of burdening someone who cares for you, or revealing your weakness or just appearing vulnerable, keeping you from reaching out for support? Who could help to lighten your load and strengthen your ability to handle it with greater resilience, courage and strength? You don't have to go it alone. Sometimes asking for help is the bravest move you can make — one that leaves everyone better off.

CHAPTER 37
Let go disappointment but retain your hope

I remember waiting anxiously for my final high-school grades to arrive in the mail. When they finally did, I was over the moon as my scores were well above those required to get into the university program I wanted to attend. When the formal university offers came out two weeks later my elation turned to disbelief: I'd missed out by one mark. I was gutted. While I got into my second preference, at another university, all my exciting plans for living in one of the residential colleges on campus fell apart and I was left to find shared accommodation through newspaper advertisements — a far cry from how I'd hoped to spend my first year living in a city far from home.

While I have to confess that there's always a part of me that wishes I'd had a chance to live in a residential college, missing out by that one mark set my life on an entirely new trajectory.

For starters, I'd never have met my husband and I likely wouldn't be writing this book right now. But there's no doubt that when hopes implode without warning, disappointment can knock us down hard.

IT'S ALWAYS TEMPTING TO SEE THINGS AS YOU WISH THEY WERE INSTEAD OF HOW THEY ARE.

Let's face it — life is full of disappointments, large and small. Sometimes the best laid plans fall apart at the seams. Sometimes people let us down. Sometimes our expectations crash to the ground with an almighty thud and our plans fall apart at the seams. As human beings, we're wired to become attached to certain outcomes, so no-one is immune to feelings of disappointment when we don't get the outcome we wanted, expected or worked hard — *really* hard — to make happen. You wouldn't be human if you didn't occasionally find the wind taken out of your sails.

The emotion of disappointment is the product of reality failing to meet with your expectations. Yet while the new reality you're confronted with may not be one you'd wanted or could ever have prepared for, it holds an invitation for you to let go your attachment to how you wished things had been and to simply accept them for how they are. Not passively or with self-pity, but with a knowing that fighting reality won't change the future, whereas accepting it will. As Scott Peck wrote in *The Road Less Travelled*, 'Life is difficult ... It is a great truth because once we truly see this truth, we transcend it'.

IF YOUR PLANS ALWAYS WORKED OUT AS YOU WANTED, YOU WOULDN'T APPRECIATE IT WHEN THEY DO.

Too often we spend so much time focused on what went wrong — on what messed up or who failed us — that we miss out on seeing new opportunities to make things go right moving forward. I'll wage a bet that some of the greatest opportunities you've ever had have emerged out the other side of a disappointment. Mine have. The truth is that if things only ever worked out as you wanted, you couldn't truly value when they did. Sure, your setbacks can set you back for a bit. But you can always use them to bounce forward more wisely, if you want. As someone once told me, everything works out in the end. If it hasn't worked out yet, then it's still not the end.

NO-ONE WILL ALWAYS ACT JUST AS YOU WANT.

It's hardly surprising that our harshest disappointments tend to involve the people we expect the most from. While we naturally expect those we're in relationships with to live by the values we aspire to ourselves — such as integrity, generosity and kindness — it doesn't mean they always will. Just as your ego sometimes gets the better of you, so too others fall prey to theirs. You can lessen your disappointment by accepting that no matter how large your efforts, how high your expectations or how desperate your hopes, you can never force the world to submit to your idea of how it should be, or force people to behave as you want.

Neuro-anatomist Jill Bolte Taylor suggests that if you sit with an emotion such as disappointment, hurt, betrayal or jealousy for 90 seconds, and really feel it fully, it washes away. While it may take more than a few minutes for you to get over your disappointment, I still encourage you to not fob it off, water it down or bury it away. Own it, acknowledge it, feel it (for at least 90 seconds!) and then let it go.

DISAPPOINTMENT TEACHES US TO LET GO OUR ATTACHMENTS. IT'S A LESSON WE RARELY LEARN QUICKLY.

Once you put your disappointment behind you, it liberates you to recalibrate your expectations, readjust your plans and then step forward with greater trust in yourself and renewed faith in your future. Life can only ever be lived in the moment. You miss the boat when you spend your days stuck with regret and resentment about what happened yesterday or with fear and anxiety about what might happen tomorrow. As for the people who have disappointed you, just trust that they have their own path to walk and lessons to learn.

Disappointments, unmet expectations, dashed hopes ... as you go through life you'll come face to face with each of them. Some people respond to them by giving up faith in their fellow human beings. Giving up pursuing their dreams. Giving up on themselves. But that's not a courageous way to respond to disappointment. Rather, your disappointments invite you to trust yourself more deeply, to keep giving your best and retain your hopes, but to let go the expectation that it will always work out the way you want. Because when you do that, you come upon opportunities to make it even better.

HOPE IS A RISK THAT MUST BE RUN

While holding on to hope may not improve your odds, giving into despair will most certainly lower them.

Sometimes letting go of our attachment to what we wanted and hoped for can take a lot more courage than we want, but it opens the window to gaining the wisdom we need for what's yet to come — to be more discerning, more adaptable, more accepting and more brave. So don't wish your disappointments away. Feel them deeply, accept them fully and be grateful for them. Sometimes not getting what you want can turn out to be a blessing in disguise as it was for me all those years ago. Either way, if not for the disappointments you've endured to now, you wouldn't be able to enjoy the times things have worked out.

Train the brave

If you are feeling disappointed right now, have the courage to trust that you're exactly where you need to be, however large the gap from where you hoped to be! Take a moment to breathe deeply. Really deeply. Right to the bottom of your stomach. As you slowly breathe out, release your disappointments from the past and anxieties for the future. Decide to just give today the best you have — for all that it is, and for all that it isn't. And remember, everything works out in the end. Let go your disappointment, but hold onto your hope.

CHAPTER 38
Do your best with what you have; it's enough

I'll never forget the moment when a visiting Swedish neurosurgeon came to my brother Frank's bedside in the rehabilitation hospital in Doha, Qatar. Twelve days earlier Frank had been out with a few mates riding his motorbike through the sand dunes outside the desert city of Doha. He'd done it many times but on this occasion he had the misfortune of riding up a dune that had a sheer 8-metre drop on the other side ... onto an unforgiving bed of rock. At the moment Frank hit that rock, the impact severely injured his spinal cord and he had to be airlifted to the hospital in Doha, where he was being stabilised while awaiting transfer back to Australia.

In the intervening 12 days, amid the fog of painkillers and between the morphine of operations, Frank had held onto hope that the paralysis he had experienced since the moment of impact would be temporary. He'd joked about walking back into that hospital one day to greet the nurses who'd been so kind to him. Cheekily, he promised to take them out dancing. Maybe even for a ride on his beloved Ducati. Frank loved to dance. He loved to ride. He loved all things outdoor.

The doctor, his eyes gentle and voice kind, stood at the foot of Frank's bed asking how he was doing. 'Not bad, Doc,' replied Frank in his cheerful way, adding, 'But I'm hoping you'll tell me some news that will make me feel better'. As kindly as he could, the doctor said, 'Frank I have looked at your scans and I think you know that this was a very serious injury. You will not walk again. However, I can tell you that after rehabilitation you will be able to have a good quality of life. So I encourage you to focus on rehabilitation rather than on trying to walk again'.

It was a brutal moment. In it, the life-changing reality of his injury hit Frank with a ferocity I'll never forget. As I held his hand, my throat tightened and I fought back my tears. I was here for my brother. This was not my time to cry.

WHEN YOU GIVE YOUR BEST, HOWEVER INSUFFICIENT IT MAY SEEM, YOU CANNOT FAIL.

Frank lay there quietly, his lifeless legs stretched out under the sheet before him. His eyes grew moist. A few tears rolled down his cheek as he stared blankly into the decades of life ahead of him. Silent minutes passed and I just held his hand. I prayed for strength, for the right words. None came. None were needed. And then Frank gave my hand a squeeze, as though to reassure me, looked over at me and said with a quiet resolve, 'I will not give this injury the power to destroy my life. It may change my life, but I will never give it the power to ruin it. There may be thousands of things I won't be able to do anymore, but there are still thousands I can and I want to do them all'.

DO THE BEST YOU CAN, WITH WHAT YOU HAVE, WHERE YOU ARE, BEGINNING NOW.

In that moment my heart swelled with immense pride, with admiration, with relief, with gratitude and with love for my big brother. In that moment, I knew without doubt that as hard as the path ahead might be for Frank, he would come through this not less than the man he'd been before, but greater.

That was in 2008. Since then Frank has lived up to his words. From scuba diving to snow skiing, from riding his bike (with customised balance wheels) through the European Alps and down the volcano craters of Bali. Time and time again he has left me and so many people in awe at his 'can-do' spirit and cheerfulness as he has worked through the many hurdles that life with paraplegia presents. But while it has slowed him down at times, and had its complications, he has never let it keep him from pursuing the things that bring him joy.

DON'T CONFINE YOURSELF TO A MENTAL WHEELCHAIR, DWELLING ON WHAT CAN'T BE DONE.

That day in the spinal injury ward, Frank reframed his circumstances to focus on what he could do, not on what he couldn't. He refused to succumb to self-pity or despair or resignation or resentment. Rather, he chose to embrace the reality of his situation without dwelling on the limitations it would impose upon him.

Of course, there are thousands of people in the world who live their lives with disabilities, some far more restricting than Frank's. After all, he can still drive a car, get on a plane and live independently. (He's on his annual scuba-diving holiday in Bali as I type!) Yet how many millions of people, whose legs work perfectly well, spend their lives confined to a mental wheelchair of their own making, forever focused on what they can't do, rather than on what they can; on what they don't have, rather than on what they do; on what isn't right, versus what is.

GIVE UP YOUR FIGHT WITH REALITY. YOU'LL NEVER WIN.

The truth is that each of us will have similar moments to the one Frank faced that day in a hospital bed in Qatar. Sure, our circumstances may differ, but the choice we face will be the same: to be held hostage by our circumstances, letting them define us, imprison us and confine us, or to get on with making the most of what's within our control.

Life can be hard, sometimes heartbreakingly so. Deciding to accept this harsh reality — rather than to fight it — is not about being passive or caving in to despair. It's simply about giving up your argument that life should be any different. Every day people around the world are diagnosed with terminal illnesses. Every day people suffer life-changing injuries. Every day people lose their jobs, their savings, their homes, and sadly, sometimes their life or that of someone they hold very dear. I don't mean to sound uncaring, cruel or harsh but ... *such is life*.

DON'T LET YOUR HARDSHIPS BECOME YOUR IDENTITY.

I'm very grateful that my brother Frank is still alive. I'm glad you are also. Because while you're alive, you have the opportunity to live every moment of your life with purpose, power and passion. Don't let your hardships and heartaches become your identity. Nor waste precious time complaining about what you can't do, don't want or don't have. Rather, spend it making the most of what you can do, using what you have to focus on what you want to create for yourself in the future. No matter how little that may feel to you in the moment, it will always — *always* — be enough.

Train the brave

Where are you dwelling on what you can't do right now instead of on what you can? Where are you surrendering power to your circumstances, letting them define you rather than focusing on what you can do to improve your situation? When you focus on what's within your power, you expand it. So give your best, even when it feels like it is far too little for the challenge at hand, and then trust that it will be enough. Because it will be.

CHAPTER 39
Anger chains you to the past; leave it there

In his book *Long Walk to Freedom,* Nelson Mandela wrote, 'As I walked out the door toward the gate that would lead to my freedom, I knew if I didn't leave my bitterness and hatred behind, I'd still be in prison'.

It was only by letting go his anger that he was able to move on with his life in a truly powerful, purposeful and dignified way and lead South Africa in writing a new chapter of history.

It would have been understandable if Mandela had left prison an angry man, after 27 years imprisonment. Many people who have suffered far less injustice than Mandela walk through life held hostage to their anger, unwilling to let it go. But at what cost? As 'unfair' as it may seem, holding on to your anger hurts you far more than anyone else. Indeed, anger (whether a grudge or a deeply held hatred toward someone) isn't good for *you.* Not good for your heart, not for your health, not for your relationships and certainly not for your happiness.

While it may not feel like it, forgiving someone for a wrong isn't about them — *it's about you*. Forgiveness is not about letting someone off the hook; it's about letting yourself off. Martin Luther King Jr. put it so beautifully when he wrote that 'Forgiveness is not an occasional act, it is a constant attitude. Forgiveness is not just a compassionate attitude towards others; it's a more compassionate attitude towards yourself'.

BE BIGGER THAN ANY WRONGS COMMITTED AGAINST YOU.

It takes courage to forgive and to let go your need to hold onto anger about something that can never be changed. However, in doing so you free yourself from the burden of anger; from that which can ultimately hurt you far more than it hurts those you refuse to forgive. Forgiveness releases the power the offending person has held over your heart, your life and your future and releases new energy into your life. Not only that, but researchers have found that forgiveness actually strengthens your immune system and your heart, and literally adds years to your life. As Mahatma Ghandi wrote, 'The weak can never forgive. Forgiveness is the attribute of the strong'.

LETTING GO OF ANGER IS LOVING YOURSELF MORE THAN YOU LOATHE SOMEONE ELSE.

Holding onto anger can weigh you down as much as walking through life with a lead ball and chain around your ankle. The act of forgiveness is about deciding that you no longer want to carry the weight from a past event into your future. It's about declaring that you love yourself more than you loathe another human being. And it's about extracting the learning, but leaving the anger behind. It simply no longer serves you ... if it ever did.

PRACTISE COMPASSION. IT WILL HELP YOU SEE THROUGH NEW EYES.

Try to put yourself in the other person's shoes — imagine how desperate, insecure, ignorant, misguided, hurt or fearful they must have felt. If nothing else, just imagine what it must be like to wake up every morning living their life. Aren't you glad you don't? Trying to understand what brought someone to behave as they did can never excuse their actions, but it can loosen the stranglehold that anger, indignation and righteousness can have on you. Always remember, hurt people hurt people. As Thomas à Kempis once wrote, 'Be assured that if you knew all, you would pardon all'.

FORGIVE YOURSELF. IT'S CHEAPER AND MORE EFFECTIVE THAN THERAPY.

It's far easier to forgive others for their mistakes, dishonesty and selfish actions when you've forgiven yourself for your own. Practising compassion for yourself — accepting your own fallibility — can help you let go grudges and avoid getting them in the first place. When you forgive yourself for being the less-than-perfect person that you are, it's possible to forgive others for their faults and failings. So if there's someone you have a particularly hard time forgiving, reflect on what it is that you must forgive yourself for before you can forgive them. Forgiving yourself is far more important than having others forgive you. In fact, it's more important than pretty much anything else at all.

FORGIVENESS DOESN'T DENY THE PAST, IT EXPANDS THE FUTURE.

Forgiveness doesn't imply that things can ever be as they once were. Nor should it. There's a distinct difference between reconciliation and forgiveness. One restores a relationship; the other simply helps you to move on without bitterness. You may have been hurt deeply, your life forever changed, your trust broken, your loyalty betrayed and your expectations dashed. So you learn to reset expectations, trust more discerningly and accept that sometimes even those you might expect the most from are no less fallible than those from whom you expect the least. Forgiving does not mean we pretend nothing hurtful ever happened. It just doesn't keep us living there.

Of course, forgiving someone who has caused you heartache can be extraordinarily hard. Forgiveness is often not a one-time event, but an ongoing commitment not to dwell on what can never be changed and to focus on creating a future that can. Yes, it takes a brave person to say sorry, but an even braver one to forgive someone who never offered an apology. Do it anyway. Not only does your heart's health depend on it, so too does your happiness.

Train the brave

Your wounds may shape who you are, but only you can decide whether to let them define who you will become. In giving up anger, you're making a declaration to yourself that you're bigger than any wrong anyone can ever commit against you. So what anger are you ready to leave in the past, enabling you to create a better future?

CHAPTER 40
Sit with your sadness

A period of great sadness in my life — and that of my family — began and ended with a phone call. I took the first one with my six-month-old daughter Madelyn on my hip. It was my mum on the other end of the phone. Her voice sounded shaken. She was speaking slowly. Too slowly. My youngest brother Peter, 20, was being detained in the Melbourne Remand Centre on robbery and assault charges. He'd been arrested by the police the day before. Twice. In one day. The first time for assaulting an elderly man and stealing his sunglasses. The second for attacking a young construction worker who was still in hospital after being injured while running away from Peter across a construction lot.

Disbelief. That's all I felt initially. Then horror. Pete, 10 years my junior, had been a bit slack when it came to his studies at university. He could be messy. He could be unreliable. But he certainly wasn't the kind of person who would beat up an elderly man or steal sunglasses off someone's head. It just couldn't be true. But the facts pointed otherwise: serious charges had been filed against him and he was locked in a jail cell.

In the days that followed we heard fragmented and incredulous stories about the mafia. How he'd been ordered to do what he did. It appeared to make sense to Pete. Not to us. A court-appointed lawyer mentioned the word 'psychotic'. They would enter an insanity defence. What? I'd heard of people going 'psycho', but it was always in the newspaper, in movies or on the evening news. Remote — in other people's worlds. It had no place in mine. Or my family's. The idea of Peter being a petty criminal seemed less harsh than him being crazy.

As awful as it was that Peter had been psychotic, we assumed this was a one-off occurrence. As my shock wore off, I felt immense faith that my youngest brother would use this experience as a valuable life lesson, one he'd eventually look back on as a profound turning point in building a successful life.

But Peter's recovery was neither smooth nor encouraging. He spent New Year's Eve of the new Millennium in a psychiatric hospital. Two months later, he was back there again. He spent his twenty-first birthday in a locked ward. Our hearts ached.

All my memories from that period are streaked red with intense anguish, sleepless nights and desperate attempts to reassure my parents it would all be okay; that he'd come out the other side of this and we just had to keep faith. After all, he was still so young, so brimming with potential and just beginning to discover the possibilities for his adult life. If he could just take a grip of his life he'd be able to turn the page on this short and shocking chapter and pursue his dreams.

Neither my family nor I had any idea at the time of what lay ahead for Peter ... or for ourselves. No idea that these hallucinations, mafia conspiracies, police paranoias and delusions were only the beginning of a severe mental illness that would ultimately rob him of ever pursuing his ambitions, isolate him from his friends, pummel his confidence and eat at the very core of his spirit. Hope was our ally, but with each relapse into psychosis, with each new 'comeback' derailed, with each encounter with the police, with each hospitalisation, it grew increasingly fragile. Still, we clung onto it with desperate hands.

And so along came the day, just over 10 years later, when the phone rang again.

It was a gorgeous spring morning when I answered the call. It was my youngest sister, Cath.

'Margie, are you sitting down?' I didn't know what was coming but my gut tightened as though I was about to be dealt a blow.

'Peter is dead,' she choked. 'He has taken his life.' In the minutes that followed, our family came together on the phone from our homes around the world. In shock and grief we tried to comprehend the incomprehensible. Our beloved brother and son, Peter, was dead. The word itself suddenly took on another dimension ... a brutal finality unlike any I'd known before.

In the decade that separated those two calls Pete had returned to psychiatric hospitals again and again, often committed in locked wards. I'd stopped counting the admissions. With each descent into madness, his dreams crashed to earth and his hopes of ever enjoying life gave way to severe paranoia, to ceaseless torment, to despair and, on the second day of April 2010, to death.

Yes, Peter was at peace at last; he would suffer no more. But oh, our beautiful brother was gone. He would never again get to shoot hoops with my kids. Never see them grow up. Never share another family celebration. Never make another one of his dry jokes. Or grow old and grey with the rest of us. And while we didn't wish him back to the tormented reality of his life, our hearts ached raw with pain that his life had ended so tragically, so brutally and so devastatingly devoid of all hope. Yes, I'd known sadness before, but not like this. This was sadness in its most painful — most heart wrenching — rawness.

WHEN WE SHUT OURSELVES OUT TO SADNESS, WE SHUT OURSELVES OUT TO JOY.

We all experience loss in our own personal way, and we should never measure one loss against another. Yet loss is loss. Grief is grief. Sadness is sadness. It comes in a million shades of black, but it's always a dark experience. There are many ways we can try to distract ourselves from the pain of loss. Eating, drinking, shopping, working, sex — they may temporarily numb the ache or bury the pain, but they can't remove it. Slowly but surely, it finds its way back to the surface.

Only when you have the courage to feel to the depth of your sadness can you be freed from it. In doing so you come to realise not only that it can't kill you, as painful as it is, but that it can connect you to a deeper dimension of living. Indeed, nothing works more potently than sadness in expanding our capacity for joy and love, for gratitude and wonder.

SADNESS POINTS US TO WHAT MATTERS MOST.

Sadness, sorrow and grief may be the hardest emotions to endure, but they're also the ones that have the most to teach us because they point us to what matters most to us in life. And only by feeling to the core of our sadness, by sitting with it and acknowledging it fully, can we connect to the deep sense of meaning that we all crave in our lives. It's why so many people who have won the battle against cancer say it's the best thing that ever happened to them. As cancer threatened them with death, it woke them up to life. There's no more precious gift.

LIVING FULLY MEANS FEELING FULLY. SOMETIMES THAT'S REALLY PAINFUL.

Living fully requires that you open your heart widely to the full gamut of human emotions. It's not about dwelling on what makes you sad, but rather about being open to feeling it when a loss triggers it within you. Only when you allow yourself to feel to the depth of your sadness can you emerge on the other side of it more whole and once again capable of feeling truly happy. Like yin and yang, you can't have one without the other.

GETTING PRESENT TO THE SADNESS THAT PULLS AT YOUR HEART IS BOTH AN ACT OF COURAGE, AND AN ACT OF SELF-LOVE.

Peter never realised the ambitions that fuelled his youth, never played professional sport, travelled the world or got to drive around in a fancy sports car. And yet his life, and the suffering he had to endure, affected the lives of those who loved him in ways we could never have imagined. He taught us to be patient; he taught us to be compassionate; he taught us not to judge those who suffer mental illness but to accept them for who they are; he taught us to love without condition and to give without expectation of return. And in the end, he taught us that life can end suddenly, but that love never does.

For that I'll be forever grateful. And as more tears find their way down my cheeks in the years to come when my family come together, less one, I offer them to the heavens, knowing that our lives, like all great masterpieces, require the darkness in order to highlight the light. Learning to sit and get fully present to all that pulls at your heart is therefore not only an act of genuine courage, it's an act of compassionate self-love. On the other side of it lies joy.

Train the brave

The gift of sadness is that it points us to pay attention to what matters most to us. It's not an emotion to be shunned or buried, but to be uncovered and felt. What events from the past, or the present, make you sad? Take some time to sit with your sadness; don't push it away. Let any tears fall. When you connect to the losses that have caused you the greatest pain you'll discover a new and deeper capacity for joy. I promise.

CHAPTER 41

Gratitude elevates; lift yourself daily

My dad often says he feels like the richest man in the world. It always makes me smile because, having been a dairy farmer his entire life, I don't think he ever earned above the minimum wage (and that would have be en a good year!). Needless to say, when he talks about feeling rich, he's not referring to the size of his pension fund (he never had one), but to the love in his life and the gratitude in his heart.

Don't get me wrong. Dad, like all people who've made it to his ripe age in life (he was born in 1935), has had his share of hardships and heartache. He lost his youngest son — my brother Peter — after a long battle with mental illness. He's supported his oldest son — my brother Frank — to adapt to life in a wheelchair after an accident left him with paraplegia. And he's endured long droughts that took all his ingenuity to find ways to feed his seven children.

Dad has taught me a lot about the power of gratitude; how it can be a tonic in difficult times and lift our spirits when we're down. Like all emotions it's contagious; like all emotions, if we feel it enough, it shapes our life. Gratitude has set up permanent residence in my dad's life and touched many others along the way. It's why I work to embrace it in my own. Admittedly, some days I fare better than others.

Of course, like any worthwhile endeavour, living with gratitude demands ongoing effort. It's so easy to get caught up focusing on all that isn't as you want it to be; what others do, or fail to do; what happening in your job or your family, with your health or your finances. If you want something to complain or worry about, you never have to look far to find it. It's why so many people spend the best years of their lives complaining and worried!

GRATITUDE TAKES NOTHING FOR GRANTED, BUT AMPLIFIES ALL THAT YOU HAVE.

Sure, life provides a constant stream of situations that don't conform to hopes and fulfil expectations. But beneath that stream runs a river of blessings that can so easily be taken for granted. Gratitude takes nothing for granted. It shines a spotlight on all that's good, amplifying its presence, all the while putting your 'problems' into perspective and emboldening you to respond to them more constructively — more courageously.

Some people mistakenly think that gratitude is an emotion best saved for when life goes to plan: when we score that goal, land that job or overcome that challenge. But gratitude has nothing to do with good fortune. We don't have to wait for something great to happen — to find the perfect partner, financial security, restored health or a bigger home — before we can practise gratitude.

GRATITUDE IS ONE OF OUR MOST MEDICINAL EMOTIONS. IT ACTS AS A TONIC FOR LIFE'S ILLS AND AILMENTS, SOOTHING OUR PAIN AND LIFTING OUR SPIRITS.

I've met people whose bodies have been crippled with arthritis, who are facing an early death because of an illness they didn't deserve or can't cure, who have lost children to wars and homes to fires and who have radiated with gratitude and a special brand of joy. How could they be so happy when life has been so hard for them? Simple. They feel grateful. I've also met people who fly around in private jets, mix with the glitterati and enjoy every luxury money can afford, yet who seem lost and forever looking for something more.

The reality is that gratitude isn't about how much or little we have, but the story we tell ourselves about it. Unleashing the power of gratitude in our daily lives therefore takes no more than recognising that life itself is a gift, that it has an expiry date and that every day—from the most pleasurable to the most anguished—is shaped by the mindset we bring to it.

I'm very grateful for many things: my four children, my good health, a loving husband, big-hearted friends and being able to do work that's deeply meaningful to me. I'm also deeply grateful for the times when life has been hard, when my heart has ached, when I've wrestled with despair and longed for certainty. I know those dark days have sewn new depth into the tapestry of my life, bringing invaluable opportunities to learn and grow in my own humanity. And I know that, over the year ahead, more will surely follow. While I don't look forward to them, I know practising gratitude will help me get through them. I know gratitude will do no less for you.

GRATITUDE EXPANDS OUR CAPACITY FOR JOY AND INFUSES A DEEPER DIMENSION INTO OUR EVERYDAY LIVING.

Of course, being in a permanent state of gratitude is a tough ask for anyone. As human beings we all succumb to the temptation of comparing and complaining and focus on what's gone wrong above what's gone right. Practising gratitude also calls us to embrace ourselves as the flawed 'human becomings' that we are. So today, instead of berating yourself when you've not appreciated the blessings of your life, decide to spread the 'gospel of gratitude' instead. After all, feeling gratitude without spreading it is like preparing a feast and not sharing it ... something my dad would never do!

Train the brave

Too often we don't appreciate what we have until we no longer have it. So take a moment to count your blessings and think about 10 things you're grateful for today, despite all that may not be just as you'd like it to be. Write them down. As Meister Eckhart wrote, 'If the only prayer you ever said in your whole life was "thank you", that would suffice'. Pray gratitude daily. Speak gratitude daily. We all need reminding.

Part V
Dare boldly

How to pursue your biggest dreams and ambitions

CHAPTER 42

Live from your imagination; not your history

When my daughter Maddy was little she used to run around the house in her diamanté tiara, pink sparkly wand in hand, pretending she was a princess with special magical powers. It brought her no end of delight making spells that would turn her three brothers into ugly toads and then, when they bowed to her royal demands or she was simply feeling magnanimous, she would turn them into handsome princes on horseback, less the horses. My sons always played along and together they'd entertain themselves for hours in an imaginary world of fairies and pirates, dinosaurs and unicorns.

Of course, by the time most of us have reached the age of double-digits, we've come to think of make-believe as child's play. All well and good for a four year old, but a childish indulgence we can ill-afford by the time we reach adulthood and grown-up concerns press in. We have careers to forge. Bills to pay. Family to support. Responsibilities to fulfil.

There's no doubt, keeping up with 'grown-up' challenges in our increasingly pressure-laden world can often leave little time or energy for imaginative play, much less outright dreaming. 'What's the point?' people often say when I ask them to imagine what their dream life would look like.

EVERY POSSIBILITY BEGINS WITH THE COURAGE TO IMAGINE.

But there is a point. The point is that before anything can be created in the world, it must first be conceived in the imagination. Likewise, before you can ever hope to live the life of your dreams, you must first imagine what it might look like. When we choose not to play make-believe and imagine what we truly yearn for — now and in the future — we cap ourselves and we cap who we can become and what we can achieve. That's not to imply the life you're living right now might not be perfectly okay. It just limits how much richer and more rewarding it could still become. As Emily Dickinson once wrote, 'The possible's slow fuse is lit by the imagination'.

Of course, letting your imagination off the leash is an act of bravery. It's brave because as soon as you allow yourself to connect with a bigger vision for your life, one that inspires you deeply, it immediately makes you vulnerable to the emotions you might feel if you fail to achieve it. Disappointment. Rejection. Humiliation. Inadequacy. Frustration. Resentment. Defeat.

LIFE IS AS BIG AS YOU DARE TO DREAM IT.

Fear of not having enough, not being enough, not doing enough and not achieving enough runs deep in our veins. So deep that it keeps many people from ever allowing themselves to dream wild, audacious dreams. But, as Michelangelo wrote, 'The greater danger for most of us lies not in setting our aim too high and falling short; but in setting our aim too low, and achieving our mark.' So, with the words of the master maestro in mind, let me ask you: What direction would your imagination soar in if you were to let it run wild and free? What would you dare to do, or achieve, or pursue, or create, or change if you were willing to dream audaciously big?

Sure, living from your imagination rather than from your history can create a vast crevasse between where you are now and where you want to be. However, life's fulfilment doesn't come from reaching any end-point destination; it comes from having the guts to work towards a goal that's bigger than you, to press on when the going gets tough and to refuse to cower to the cynics or setbacks. As I wrote earlier in this book, one of life's greatest prizes is working hard at work worth doing, regardless of whether you achieve what you set out to do.

IF YOUR BIGGEST GOALS ARE EASILY REACHED, THEN YOU'RE THINKING TOO SMALL.

Yitzhak Rabin didn't create the peace he wanted between Israel and the Palestinian people. Mother Teresa didn't end the injustice of the underprivileged in India. Martin Luther King Jr. didn't end racism. Bill Gates has yet to eradicate polio or end malaria (although the Gates Foundation he created is getting closer). But each of these people, in daring to do what some would have said was impossible, have left an indelible mark upon the world because they had the courage to dream bravely and dare boldly. Which leaves me with a question: Where do you need to dream bigger dreams?

Train the brave

To make your dreams come true you must first be brave enough to have them. This requires letting your imagination run free. So put aside your adult sensibilities right now and imagine you're holding your very own magic wand which, with a lot of hard work, could grant you whatever you wanted. Then imagine it's 10 years from now and put yourself in the shoes — in the everyday life — of you plus 10 years. Visualise yourself in a place that you know well or would like to know better, living a life that truly inspires you. If you can, get someone to read out these questions to you as you close your eyes and let your imagination take flight. Afterwards, write down whatever appeared in your mind's eye. Don't let it escape you. It appeared for a reason.

» Where are you living?

» How old are you? How old is your partner and/or children?

» How do you start your day? How do you end it?

» What are you doing each day?

» Who are you doing it with?

» Whose lives would you be touching because of who you are and how you work, live and lead?

» What challenges are you pursuing?

» What value are you adding?

» What relationship do you have with money?

» What skills and strengths are you building?

» What are you not doing, delegating or outsourcing?

» What conversations are you engaged in … with whom … about what?

» What kind of relationship do you enjoy with your family, friends, co-workers and others around you?

» What emotions do you feel about yourself and your future?

» How do you feel physically? How do you look physically?

» What are your proudest accomplishments of the past decade?

» What would you like to tell the person reading this today?

CHAPTER 43

Pave your own path

One day in my early teen years my dad said to me, 'Margaret Mary, I see great things for you'.

'Do you, Dad?' I asked, my eyes wide and brimming with anticipation as images of celebrities and trailblazers flashed through my mind. Whitney Houston. Margaret Thatcher. Princess Diana! It wouldn't have taken much to say something that sounded exciting to a farm girl whose horizons extended little further than the back paddock or local football grounds.

'I see you being Sister Margaret Mary,' he said, 'in charge of a convent'.

My shoulders slumped and my face dropped. I felt like a balloon that had collided with the pointy end of my grandma's knitting needle. I let out an indignant sigh and gave Dad the biggest eye-roll I could muster before storming off. I suspect he knew it was a long shot but couldn't resist the temptation to offer it up.

While I never felt seriously pressured to become a nun, I've met hundreds of people who have pursued careers based on what they felt they 'should' do, not on what they wanted to do. Some have wanted to be teachers, but were steered down the path of law. Others wanted to be nurses, but were steered towards business. Some wanted to do business, but were pressured to study medicine, like three generations had before them.

Some people have had the fortitude to go their own way from the outset and deal with the familial fallout. Others I've known have made the bold decision to change course midway, despite having already travelled a considerable distance down the path others (often parents) wanted for them. But many people I've known — too many — haven't. Too risky. Too late. Too hard. Too much invested to start over again. Instead they stick to a path that brings them little joy on the bet that doing so will afford them the freedom to change paths later on.

Of course, you may not necessarily be on the wrong path. You may in fact be on the right one. But perhaps how you're going about it each day isn't working for you and has been overly influenced by the opinions of others.

SOMETIMES FINDING THE RIGHT PATH FIRST REQUIRES GETTING A LITTLE LOST.

We all have to find our own path and no-one can find it for us — not even those who know you best or love you most! Sure, some may point you in the right direction and there may be people whose lives have inspired you, but there's no-one with your unique combination of skill, talent, interest, experience, opportunity and personal preference. Just because a particular path has worked for them, doesn't mean it's right for you. And just because you can't see a clear path ahead doesn't mean you shouldn't start walking in the direction that calls to you. Sometimes you have to risk getting a little lost before you can find the path that's right for you. I've felt a little lost many times myself.

Sometimes we can also fall into the trap of thinking that we should make the same decisions, and follow the same paths, as those of our role models, mentors and 'heroes', both living and dead. Not true. The context of your life is different, the concerns you have are different and *you are different!*

The line from Robert Frost's famous poem regarding taking the road less travelled has earned its fame for a reason. It strikes at the choices we must all make through life ... to stay on the path of the familiar, or to diverge on the one less travelled.

As tempting as it can be to follow along the same path as others you've seen go before you, at some point in life you'll find that being true to yourself demands that you venture bravely onto unknown ground and pave your own path. While going your own way — which may take you away from the crowd you've been hanging with — can be scary, it's when you have the courage to venture into uncertain territory that you discover a whole new world of possibility that would otherwise have remained out of sight. So, if you don't like the path you're walking, pave a new one. And if some people don't understand why you venture off the path you're on, they don't need to. It's not for them.

Train the brave

Give yourself some time away from others to ask yourself what it is you really want — and I mean really, *really, REALLY* want. Keep asking yourself that question until you bury down to the heart of what it is you truly yearn for most in life. Freedom. Peace. Love. Acceptance.

(continued)

Train the brave *(cont'd)*

There's no right or wrong answer. But once you find it, ask yourself, 'Where do I need to change what I'm doing and pave my own path?' There will be plenty of obstacles that line the path you want to take. Just don't make yourself be one of them.

CHAPTER 44

Yes, take that chance! The odds are better than you think

Take a moment to look back on your life to date and think about when you could have been more courageous and less cautious — in your work, your relationships or elsewhere in your life. I'm sure you can recall at least a few situations where, with the benefit of hindsight, you wished you'd acted more courageously, taken a bigger risk, settled less or dared more. If so, then just know you aren't alone.

Of course, hindsight is a wonderful thing. 'If only I knew then what I know now' we say to ourselves as we lament the times we played it safe rather than taking the plunge, held our tongue rather than speaking up, took the easier path rather than the less certain one. But here's the deal: the same invisible forces that drove you to play it safe back then are still in action right now and impacting the future ahead of you.

KNOWING YOUR COGNITIVE BIASES WILL HELP YOU COMPENSATE FOR THEM.

When it comes to training the brave within you, it's vital to first be aware of your own cognitive biases. Or, put another way, the unconscious tendencies you have that can undermine your decision-making logic. While human beings have always had these biases, new advances in brain-imaging technology have been able to identify four different ways we're wired to avoid taking the risks that would ultimately make us happier.

The fact is that most of us are pretty lousy when it comes to weighing up the risks and assessing the odds. Further, the more emotional we feel about a decision, the more biased and less accurate we are. While you may never rewire your brain's ability to assess risk, by becoming aware of how it steers you away from risk and towards caution you can see more clearly where you need to do the very thing that scares you.

POTENTIAL LOSSES LOOM LARGER THAN GAINS.

We're wired to focus more on what might go wrong — what we might lose — than on what might go right — what we could gain. This causes us to overestimate the probability of things going wrong and underestimate the chances of them working out in our favour. As Nobel laureate Daniel Kahneman wrote in *Thinking, Fast and Slow,* 'People overestimate the probabilities of unlikely events. Potential losses tend to loom larger than potential gains'.

When I set about writing my first book, *Find Your Courage,* I would have dreams of picking up *The New York Times* and seeing my face and book cover blazoned across the front page with the headline 'World's Worst Book'. The reality is that even if I did write the world's worst book (which would have been quite a feat in itself!), it would never have scored a mention in *The New York Times*, much less have been given front-page coverage!

This is what I referred to in that same book as 'catastrophising'. We come up with dire, dramatic and usually wildly unrealistic worst-case scenario images in our mind's eye. Rather than assume that we would act quickly to head off or mitigate a situation if things started going off track, we imagine everything spiralling shockingly out of control while we stand passively by, powerless to do anything and destined for destitution and social humiliation. Okay, maybe you don't catastrophise quite as dramatically as me, but you must still be careful not to let your fear of what could go wrong keep you from doing what could make things more right.

DON'T UNDERESTIMATE YOUR ABILITY TO HANDLE RISKS.

Hand in hand with this, we often underestimate our own ability to handle the challenges we face — whether things go wrong or right! And ladies, we out-do men on this front. By doubting ourselves too much, and backing ourselves too little, we veer away from taking on or pursuing bigger challenges.

Lynn Kraus, managing partner of Ernst & Young's Sydney office, shared with me how she had declined an offer to take on the senior leadership role several times before finally accepting. Each time she'd turned it down, it was because she didn't think she had the ability to succeed in the position. Looking back now, with the benefit of having been in the role for several years, Lynn realised that she'd been gravely underestimating herself. Fortunately for her, those who saw her potential didn't give up on her easily. But still, how often do we sell ourselves short and steer away from opportunities and aspirations because we doubt our ability to handle them? In my experience, far too often.

Our cognitive biases — to overestimate the probability of things going wrong, to underestimate ourselves and to discount the cost of inaction — explain why so many capable people find themselves living in such a restricted circle of their potential: dissatisfied in their careers, stuck in their relationships and living lives they would never consciously have chosen.

To quote futurist Alvin Toffler: 'It is better to err on the side of daring than the side of caution'. So take that chance. Make that change. Pursue that dream. The odds are better than you think.

Train the brave

No-one likes to lose a bet, but unless you take a bet on the future you want, you're guaranteed not to get it. So as you look towards your future, ask yourself:

» Where is my aversion to risk holding me back?

» Where is my fear of not achieving what I want getting in the way of me going after it?

» What is the worst thing I'm afraid might happen?

» How likely is it to happen and what would I do to intervene if it started to?

» How will I feel a year from now if I do nothing?

» What can I do right now to increase the odds of my success in the big game of life? (Note to self: playing safe and avoiding risks is not the answer!)

CHAPTER 45

Fear regret more than failure

Young, idealistic and naïve. These words describe Justine Flynn and her three university friends when they came up with what they felt was a great idea. They would sell bottled water to help fund wells and water systems to provide safe drinking water for people in other parts of the world who had to spend hours each day carrying buckets to get it otherwise. The only challenge was they had between them little money, no experience and no idea how to do it. While they knew it would probably not be easy, they were determined they would never look back and wonder, 'What if?' So they set off to make it happen.

'We had an idea, we had passion, but apart from that, not much else,' Justine told me when I interviewed her for Raw Courage TV. It took jumping a few thousand hurdles, encountering numerous naysayers (including those who told them getting national distribution for their drink would be 'absolutely impossible'), but eventually they did it! Today Thankyou Water is sold in more than 4000 stores across Australia alongside its other products including Thankyou Food. But the real measure of success is in the fact that sales have funded nearly 5000 water solutions in 13 countries giving well over 100 000 people access to drinking water. Which just goes to show, sometimes being young, idealistic and naïve about getting an idea off the ground can be a very good thing.

The reality is that many people don't want to risk the failure, the rejection, the setbacks or the struggles that are all part and parcel of achieving something really worthwhile. In the book *The Five Regrets of the Dying,* written by palliative care nurse Bronnie Ware, there was no mention of more sex or free-diving by the patients in her care as they reflected back on their lives. Nor of faster cars, big homes or fewer children. Rather, facing their imminent death, her patients just said that they wished they had expressed their feelings more often, held fewer grudges and been more open to change. The most common regret of all was this:

'I wish I'd had the courage to live a life true to myself, not the life others expected of me'.

It's a sentiment I've heard time and time again by people as they look back on their lives and reflect on the choices they made, and those they were too afraid to make. It's not that most people are sorry that they weren't able to accomplish their ambitions or achieve their dreams. It's that they regretted not even having tried. The clarity of vision that comes when facing the end enabled them to see that they had let their fear of falling short or losing face keep them from living their lives fully; of being true to themselves.

AT LIFE'S END, PEOPLE DON'T REGRET THE RISKS THEY TOOK; THEY REGRET THOSE THEY DIDN'T.

Too often, our fear of not being able to succeed keeps us from ever starting out. But it's in daring to attempt something for which we have no guarantee of success that our lives are transformed; not in the victory itself. As I've seen time and time again, when you have the courage to start out towards a long-held dream, you learn more about what it takes to achieve it, you discover new strengths and talents you didn't know you had, and you open up new opportunities and possibilities in your life that you can't even imagine existed before you began your adventure.

The dreams that have always inspired you are unique to you. No-one on planet Earth is drawn towards the exact same set of dreams, ambitions, aspirations and opportunities. Nor does anyone have the same unique combination of talents, passion, personality and experience to pursue them. Use yours to do something no-one else can. Life's not difficult because we dare too much; it's difficult because we dare too little.

BE CAREFUL NOT TO LET YOUR FEAR OF WHAT YOU DON'T WANT KEEP YOU FROM PURSUING WHAT YOU DO.

And yes, there's no guarantee that you'll achieve what you set out to do. But you're absolutely guaranteed never to reach it if you stay at home watching *Friends* re-runs. There are thousands of people living in Laos, Haiti, Uganda, Bangladesh, Myanmar, East Timor, Burundi and numerous other countries, who now have ready access to fresh, drinkable water they didn't have before, thanks to Justine and her Thankyou co-founders.

Everything worthwhile I've ever done has required a thousand steps outside my comfort zone. While not every risk has paid off, I've never regretted taking one. Not once. The only things I'm at all regretful about is when I have let my fear of disapproval, rejection, being inadequate or making a fool of myself keep me from even trying.

The truth is that the more often you put yourself 'out there' — the more doors you knock on, the more people you meet, the more times you try — the more doors of opportunity will open for you. You won't always know which ones will work out, but rest assured, if you keep stepping out of your comfort zone toward the goals and dreams that inspire you, you will eventually find yourself in a place far more rewarding and exciting than you could have ever imagined before you started out. The key: fear regret more than you fear failure.

Train the brave

Imagine yourself in the final days of your life and looking back on the journey you've travelled. If you keep on the same path you're on right now, avoiding the same risks you've avoided until now, what is it that you might regret not doing? Whatever comes to mind, write it down and then share it with someone you love. Just doing that will bring new life to your dream. The other chapters in this book will help you to turn it into reality.

CHAPTER 46

Break the rules; make your own

It's a well-worn saying that rules are meant to be broken. Not all the time and not every time. Rules do, of course, serve a purpose. They bring structure to our lives and order to our society. However, like all things in life, blindly doing something because we're told we 'should' and not because we can see how it genuinely makes sense or serves us and the world at large, is never a good reason to do it. Which is why, as useful as rules can be, there are times we need to have the courage to break them.

One of my favourite rule breakers is Rosa Parks who, by daring to break the rules, set off a movement that changed a nation. On 1 December 1955, Rosa, a 42-year-old African-American seamstress, boarded a Montgomery City bus to go home from work. She sat near the middle of the bus, just behind the 10 seats reserved for white people. Soon all of the seats in the bus were filled. When a white man got on the bus, the driver (following the standard practice of segregation) insisted that all four African-Americans sitting just behind the white section give up their seats so that the man could sit there.

In a moment that would live forever in history, Rosa made a snap decision to defy the rules. That one act of courageous rebellion — not just against the rules of her society at the time, but the rules of the land — triggered the Montgomery Bus Boycott, which spearheaded a new era in America's quest for racial equality.

Of course, from our vantage point in history it's easy to agree that Rosa Parks did the right thing by breaking the rules. But, let's face it, many people wouldn't have. While we don't all feel compelled to break the rules governing our organisation or society, throughout our lives we'll each be called to defy the rules and traditions of those around us in some way, large or small.

SOMETIMES BRAVERY CALLS FOR REBELLION.

Too often we let the 'rules' — both explicit and unwritten — dictate *what* we do, *how* we do it and *who* we become in the process. Blindly and compliantly living by rules that keep us from fulfilling our deepest needs and desires (assuming we aren't narcissists or psychopaths) doesn't serve anyone. Here are some of the rules people have shared with me which, at the time, were not serving them, but which they were following anyway for fear of violating a social, organisational or family norm:

» You *must* do what your boss says, no matter what.

» You *must* attend regular networking events.

» You *must* send your children to private schools.

» You *must* follow tradition.

» You *must* spend at least two years in a job before moving on.

» You *must* eat what's on your plate and never decline a drink.

- » You *must* find a secure career path.
- » You *must* respect your parents' wishes, no matter what.
- » You *must* stay in your marriage, no matter what.

When people tell me I 'simply must' do something (such as sign my kids up for some class, join an association or buy some new software program), it's a sure sign I don't really have to. As Tina Fey wrote in her book *Bossypants*, 'No one says "You must give birth to a baby when you go into labour", because when you really must do something, you don't need to say it!'

Of course, some of these 'musts' and 'shoulds' (aka 'rules') may seem ridiculous to you, but rest assured there are plenty of people who live their lives according to a long list of unwritten rules. When I hear people make statements such as these, I can't help but respond with 'Says who?'

GAME CHANGERS ARE RULE BREAKERS.

Thomas Edison, the man who brought electricity to the masses, once said, 'Heck there are no rules here. We're trying to accomplish something'. The people who change the world are those who refuse to play by the rules. If you look at the companies today that are breaking new ground, you'll find they're the ones being steered by leaders who refuse to follow the old rules of business management, marketing or anything else. YouTube broke the rule that videos are meant for the television screen. Amazon broke the rule that people only want books they can hold in their hand. Dell broke the rule that people only wanted to buy their electronics in stores. And Apple? They have totally rewritten the rule books. As Steve Jobs once said, 'The people [rule breakers] who are crazy enough to think that they can change the world, are the ones who do'.

WE MUST REGULARLY QUESTION THE RULES THAT GOVERN OUR LIVES, LEST THEY RULE US.

Rules should ultimately expand your freedom to live the life you want, not restrict it. So whether it's how you're taking your products to market, managing your team, raising your children or running your social life, be mindful that in order to pursue the biggest life you truly want to live, you'll sometimes have to break the rules. That doesn't mean there won't be a fallout or that everyone will be happy with you, but don't kid yourself about the cost of compliance. All that truly matters is that you don't become an unwitting victim of the 'musts' and 'must nots' of those around you.

You know it's time to break your own rules when your desire to make yourself happy grows larger than your desire to keep others happy. So before you renew the contract, buy the house, spend the money or make one more big decision, take a moment to check in with your inner sage and ask yourself, 'Is this what I truly want to do, or am I simply afraid of the consequences of choosing something else?'

General Douglas MacArthur once said, 'You are remembered by the rules you break'. It takes courage to live life on your own terms, to resist the pressure to comply with the rules others want you to live by and to meet the expectations they have for you. Start by breaking some small rules and build from there.

Make your *own* plans. Chart your *own* course. Express your *own* style. Speak your *own* thoughts. Build your *own* life — and when the rules others are working and living by confine you, make your own! Life's too short to be lived by anyone's rules but your own. Sometimes bravery calls for rebellion!

Train the brave

Where are you living by the rules, expectations and desires of those around you, rather than by your own deepest desires? Which rules do you need to break in order to live the life *you* really want?

CHAPTER 47
Forget perfect! Good enough is good enough

Speaking at a medical conference to a room full of surgeons, I was comforted when hundreds of hands went up after I asked who considered themselves a perfectionist. When it comes to operating on my body, fixing the brakes in my car or laying the foundation on my home, I'm all for keeping the bar really high. But given the culture of perfectionism that we live in today, we need to discern between when aiming for perfectionism is serving us and others and when it's not.

In writing this book I've sometimes felt inadequate for the task. I want to write a book that will embolden you to become braver in your work, your relationships and your life. However, I'm well aware of my limitations, my lousy grammar and that I have none of the literary genius of some writers whose books line my shelves. But I write anyway because I know that if I waited until I had a Shakespearean command of the English language, it would never be written. And so I swallow my fear of falling short, embrace my vulnerability and continue typing, all the while reminding myself of one of my favourite life maxims: Done is better than perfect.

DONE IS BETTER THAN PERFECT.

As you read this now, I'm guessing there may be things you'd also like to do that you haven't because you don't feel you're skilled, or knowledgeable, or capable enough to perform at the level of mastery or success that you'd like. At least not quickly enough!

Let's face it, it's only natural to aspire to do things in a way that makes us proud and others impressed. But you rarely need to do things perfectly to do them as well as they need to be done. Aspiring to attain the highest standards in every endeavour and domain of life can leave you stuck on the perfectionist's merry-go-round, forever striving, but going continually in circles and never arriving at an end point. Because when it comes to attaining and maintaining perfectionism — in our work, our bodies, our homes and our lives — it's an elusive quest. In most matters of life, *good enough is good enough*, particularly if perfectionism keeps it from ever being done!

PERFECTIONISM CAN CONFINE PEOPLE TO A LIFE OF IMMACULATE MEDIOCRITY.

Our desire to have things 'just perfect' can drive people to continually *do* more, *be* more and *have* more, but never feeling like it's enough. Left unchecked, perfectionism can leave us living lives of immaculate mediocrity, spending too much time on things that don't matter and too little on things that do. So, whether it's the interior design of your living room or the formatting of PowerPoint slides you're working on, ask yourself, 'Is this the best use of my time right now? How is it keeping me from more important tasks and aspirations?' There are things that only you can do, but they will never be done if you're pre-occupied with perfecting less important things.

AIMING FOR 'PERFECT' WILL LEAVE YOU ALWAYS STRIVING, NEVER ARRIVING.

Perfectionism puts us on a merry-go-round, forever striving but never arriving. Since we can never be good enough for long enough, perfectionism never lets us rest as we kill ourselves trying to live up to some idealised standard. Most of all, it keeps us from ever trying to do many of the things we'd love to do, for fear of not doing them well enough. As Brené Brown wrote in *The Gift of Imperfection*, 'Perfectionism hampers success'.

PERFECTIONISM IS THE MOTHER OF PROCRASTINATION.

The fact is that, right now you're plenty good enough to get started towards accomplishing new goals and pursuing new dreams. It begins with being brave enough to trust that what you have right now is all you need to get started. Perfectionism not only kills dreams, but it stifles potential and limits success. It is the mother of procrastination. And so whatever it is that you yearn for most, know this: You're smart *enough*, strong *enough*, worthy *enough*, capable *enough*, good *enough* and brave *enough* right now. Just as you are. As imperfect as you are!

Just think about how many adults who never learned to swim as children refuse to learn as adults. Their fear of having to go through the same learning curve that every child does keeps them from parking their pride and getting in the pool! Don't fall into that same trap when it comes to doing something that would expand your experience of life.

Rather, put your hand on your heart, take a big, deep breath (yes, seriously, do it!) and then just trust in yourself that you have everything it takes to do what you really want to do. What you don't yet know, you'll learn. And what you can't do well won't matter. You were born to be real, not to be perfect.

Train the brave

Perfect is the enemy of done. It's action, not perfectionism, that helps you move forward to living your greatest life. So how might giving up having to do something perfectly help you step more powerfully into action towards your greatest aspirations? What would you start doing and what would you stop doing? Remember, good enough is good enough!

CHAPTER 48

Embrace problems that are worthy of you

The hinges on my oven door are loose. My filing cabinet needs sorting. One of my sons has handwriting that is bordering on illegible. Another child needs new school shoes (again!). The gas bill needs paying. My car needs servicing. And I've yet to file my taxes (if you happen to work for the tax office, I can assure you they will be!).

If right about now you're thinking to yourself, *booooring* then you'd be right. That's exactly what it is. It's not that I don't have to address these 'problems'; it's just that in the larger game of life they're mundane, repetitious, tiny blips on the radar.

The bigger problem for many people is how easily we can allow these mundane 'first-world' problems to dominate our lives. To be honest, as I listed down my 'problems' above, it made me squirm. I really don't want to give them any more energy than the very minimum required to address them. Book the service. Pay the bill. File the taxes. Yada yada yada.

BE CAREFUL YOU DON'T INFLATE SMALL PROBLEMS INTO BIG ONES.

Of course, I use the word 'problems' loosely. There's a distinct difference between having big problems and making your problems big. Too often we get caught in a trap of amplifying the small, petty problems of our life into big ones. Which wouldn't be a problem except that it can keep us living in the petty minutia of life and prevent us from taking on bigger (more exciting and meaningful) problems that would not only make us feel more alive, but would put all the small ones in perspective.

Mastery of life is not the absence of problems, it's the mastery of problems. People who are living big, rewarding lives aren't continually trying to avoid problems; they're forever chasing bigger ones.

TAKING ON BIG PROBLEMS PUTS ALL YOUR OTHER PROBLEMS INTO PERSPECTIVE.

Albert Einstein once said, 'Problems cannot be solved by the same level of thinking that created them'. Likewise, when you enlarge the lens through which you view your problems it reframes formerly pressing problems into petty ones and expands your capacity to handle everyday problems that flow in and out of your life with more humour and less angst. Instead of resisting your problems and complaining, 'Things shouldn't be this way!' ask 'How can I make things better?'

Sheryl Sandberg has been a powerhouse in encouraging women to lean in. Malala Yousafzai is working tirelessly to ensure *all* girls have access to the education they need to thrive. And there are countless other people you and I have never heard of who are spending their lives working to solve the big problems we face on this planet. Will they succeed? We can't know. What I do know is that by having the courage to embrace big problems, to pursue massive goals and to take on lofty aspirations, their lives are exponentially richer, deeper and broader than they would otherwise be.

Imagine the world today if the Wright brothers had stuck with repairing bicycles rather than solving the larger problem of defying the law of gravitational pull. If Henry Ford had just tried to engineer a faster horse buggy. If Steve Jobs had decided to retire to the golf course after being sacked from Apple. If Sara Blakely had not invented Spanx! It's unthinkable!

You may not feel inspired to invent the next iPhone, but you were born with a unique set of innate talents and have since acquired a unique set of skills and knowledge. Don't go to your grave without honouring what you have, who you are and your ability to leave your own unique mark on the world.

While travelling in Cambodia recently I heard an old Laotian saying: 'If you like things easy, you'll have difficulties; if you like problems you'll succeed'. Likewise, you can generally tell the size of a person by the size of their problems. Whether it's taking on the problems that will line the path to pursuing a huge goal, or it's taking on the problems that limit the lives of others, have the courage to take on problems that are worthy of you.

Train the brave

Creating a more rewarding life begins by seeing your problems through a larger lens: viewing small problems for what they are and embracing bigger ones for what they will call you to be.

Where are you spending too much time focusing on small problems, amplifying the space they take up in your life by complaining about them and treating them as though they shouldn't exist? In the space that opens up, ask yourself, 'What bigger problems would I be truly inspired to focus on instead?'

CHAPTER 49
Courage is contagious; walk with giants

There have been plenty of times over the years when I've found myself feeling a little (or a lot) out of sorts, unsure of myself and the best way forward. Sometimes I've just needed a listening ear to vent a frustration. Other times I've needed someone to bounce an idea off, to challenge my thinking, or help me figure out the best way forward. And other times, I've simply wanted a word of encouragement; a reminder to keep faith in myself and my dreams.

ISOLATION IS A DREAM KILLER.

Having people to lean on during those times has made a profound difference in my life. In fact, I think it's fair to say you wouldn't be reading this book now if I hadn't been able to lean on the support of others when I needed it. By sharing your journey with others, those you travel with can help you navigate the obstacles you face, pick you up when you fall, lend you their courage when yours is low and point you in the right direction when you're lost. And let's face it, there are times when we can all lose our bearings. Isolation is a dream killer.

That said, if you're hanging with people who aren't much into dreaming, you may find the going tough. I'm guessing you've heard the saying 'you become the company you keep'. That's because you can't help but be shaped by the values, outlook and emotions of those you spend time with. You unconsciously adopt an outlook of those around you, which includes their assumptions about what's possible for you, and often more importantly, what isn't.

YOU BECOME THE COMPANY YOU KEEP. CHOOSE WISELY.

If you want to live a really rewarding life, be deliberate about who you spend your time with because, like it or not, the people who surround you shape how you see the world, which in turn shapes the life you create and the person you become ... for better or worse.

Emotions are highly contagious, so the interaction you have with other people impacts your emotional state. The Longevity Project, which studied more than 1000 people from youth to death, found that the groups you associate with often determine the type of person you become. For instance, if you hang out with people who are very health conscious and value staying active, you're more likely to be a healthy, active person yourself. And if you're part of a group of people who are ambitious and have a strong work ethic, you're more likely to become successful yourself. On the flip side, if you hang with a crowd that has few aspirations, you'll find it does little to encourage your own. It's hard to soar like an eagle if you're hanging out with turkeys.

If you surround yourself with people who are constantly encouraging you and sometimes seem to believe in you even more than you do yourself, you'll know what a huge impact those people can make. As Charles Duhigg wrote in his book *The Power of Habit*, 'When people join groups where change seems possible, the potential for that change to occur becomes more real'.

SOMETIMES WE NEED TO LET GO OF OLD FRIENDSHIPS TO MAKE ROOM FOR BETTER ONES.

Good friendships can enrich your life immeasurably and help you ride the waves during tough times. Sometimes though, we can fall into 'friendship ruts', spending time with people we've known 'forever' and lingering in relationships that, while comfortably familiar, can hold us back.

In *Harry Potter and the Philosopher's Stone*, J.K. Rowling wrote that 'It takes a great deal of bravery to stand up to our enemies, but just as much to stand up to our friends.' If you often feel disempowered and lacking energy after spending time with certain people, it may be time to 'prune your tree' in order to create the space to nurture new relationships. Leaving the familiarity of old relationships and stepping into the uncertainty of those yet to be made takes courage. But you have to ask yourself, will staying in these relationships set you up to build the life you want 5, 10 or 25 years from now? Have the courage to act on the answer.

SURROUND YOURSELF WITH PEOPLE YOU WANT TO BE MORE LIKE.

Surround yourself with people who are living the values you aspire to live by yourself. Surround yourself with people who engage in big conversations about things that matter to you. Surround yourself with people who believe you're capable of whatever you set your mind to and who will support you in doing whatever it takes to achieve it. And finally, surround yourself with people who you know care about you achieving and becoming all that inspires you more than they care about the possibility that you may leave them behind.

When you surround yourself with people who believe in you, it infuses you with the optimism, confidence and courage needed to achieve what you want, and to ride the waves when the going gets tough. When you walk with big people — with big hearts and brave dreams — you'll become bigger yourself. So walk with giants.

Train the brave

Imagine how differently you'd feel, think and act if you only spent time with big-thinking, big-living, big-hearted people. Given how profoundly people can impact your self-confidence, outlook and actions, write down the names of five people you'd like to spend more time with and then reach out to make that happen. Not only will you be better off, so will they!

CHAPTER 50

Think big; start small; begin now

Having a deeply meaningful dream, goal or aspiration to work towards can profoundly shift your day-to-day experience of life. Whether it be building a business, raising your children, forging a career or climbing your own personal Everest, knowing what you want to achieve can help guide your day-to-day choices and infuse your life with a new sense of meaning and purpose. However, about two seconds after getting inspired, many people (like me!) go into immediate overwhelm.

> ***Where to start? How to proceed? What if I can't? What if I fail? Maybe I'm kidding myself that I can do this.***

Self-doubt can quickly wrestle ambition to the ground. While you may want to achieve something really huge that leaves you quivering at the knees, you can do yourself a big disservice if you try to bite off too much of the apple with your first bite. So, if you're overwhelmed at the thought of all that's involved in achieving a goal that feels massive, start by breaking it down. That is, break your big, lofty vision down into smaller, less daunting, shorter term goals and then into smaller, more doable, bite-sized steps.

COMMIT TO ONE STEP AT A TIME, HOWEVER SMALL THAT STEP MAY SEEM.

Starting small is how I wrote my first book, *Find Your Courage*. While I was passionate about the message I wanted to share (and still am), I had four children under the age of seven at the time. To combat overwhelm, I set myself a goal of writing the outline in 12 months, which broke it down to one chapter outline a month. The irony is that by taking the pressure off myself, I ended up actually writing nine chapters during that time. Likewise, if you find yourself moving into overwhelm, focus on what you want to do in the next day, or week.

Write down whatever actions you're committed to taking, with a deadline against each one — however seemingly small, mundane or insignificant they may be. Then schedule the time to do them. Then next week, do the same thing. Repeat as often as necessary! Over time you grow the skills, knowledge and mastery needed to get you where you want to go. Don't wait until you know everything before you start doing something.

EMBRACE DISCOMFORT. YOU'LL NEVER THRIVE IN YOUR COMFORT ZONE.

Nothing worthwhile is achieved by staying inside your comfort zone and sticking to what you know you can do well; that is, what you're guaranteed to succeed at. Feeling the discomfort that comes from stepping up to the plate in life to try to do something you've never done before is part and parcel of what it takes to succeed at anything. Embrace it. Over time the things that once felt really scary and uncomfortable become less so.

Achieving anything truly worthwhile takes continual and focused effort, particularly at the beginning when you're trying to build momentum. An aeroplane has to use an enormous amount of its fuel (up to 25 per cent) just to get off the tarmac and into the air. Likewise, for you to make a change in your life, or to get some serious momentum going towards achieving a big ambition, it's going to take a lot more energy — mental, emotional, physical and spiritual — up front than may seem reasonable. Don't assume everything you do will fall into place (it rarely does) and don't pressure yourself into doing everything today, or this week, or this month, or even this year. Just keep putting one foot in front of the other, taking one step at a time, one day at a time, continually reconnecting with what inspired you to take action in the first place. Over time, the path you need to take will become more and more obvious.

EVERY GREAT ACCOMPLISHMENT IS THE RESULT OF A THOUSAND SMALL BRAVE STEPS.

So think big, start small and begin now. Inaction fuels self-doubt. Action fuels the confidence to rise above it. The next chapter of your life begins the moment you make the decision to begin your journey. Your greatest dreams and deepest yearnings are riding on it.

Train the brave

Identify the first 10 steps you need to take in the next seven days to start you on your way to achieving a goal that's really meaningful to YOU! Schedule time for each step. Do at least one thing daily. Then schedule time a week from now to repeat the process again.

Epilogue

At the beginning of this book I suggested that it wasn't a book to be read in a sequential order. As such, it has no end. Which is fitting really, because living bravely doesn't either. Embracing your vulnerability and choosing to live more bravely, speak more bravely, love more bravely and dare more bravely is something you're called to do until your final breath. So rather than relating to bravery as a virtue to practise from time to time, think of bravery as something to infuse into every corner of your life, every choice you make and every step you take. That's when you'll be at your most powerful.

BE BOLD, BE BRAVE, BE FEARLESS … EVEN IF YOU'RE NOT. LIFE REWARDS ACTION.

Of course, this whole living bravely concept is much easier said than done. I know because while I write and talk and live and breathe the message of courage, I'm not immune to fear and can sometimes cower to it. Which is why I also don't pretend to offer you a 10-step magic formula for becoming brave.

The truth is that neither this book — nor, for that matter, any book — can make you brave. Only you can. You'll do it by making the decision, again and again and again, not to let fear hold the balance of power in your life, but to trust yourself more deeply, to own your fears and then to step boldly, purposefully, through it — however uncomfortable or outright terrifying that may be. And every time you fall and fail — which you will — you'll forgive yourself for being human, get back up, brush yourself off and begin anew. Just as a single step on earth doesn't make a new path, so too a single thought won't make a new pathway in your mind. To become truly brave, you must choose to think the brave thoughts that you want to dominate your life.

AS YOU REFUSE TO LET DOUBT DICTATE YOUR CHOICES, NEW DOORS OF OPPORTUNITY WILL OPEN. JUST WAIT!

None of us can rewind the clock to make a brand new start. But every single day of your life offers you the opportunity to begin to create a brand new end — an end that honours all that you've experienced, all that you are and all that you aspire to be. Today is one of them. The catch (yes, sorry, there's always a catch!) is that you have to park the excuses that have been keeping you small and begin telling yourself new stories that call you powerfully into purposeful and bold action.

SOMETIMES THE HARDEST PART OF THE JOURNEY IS BELIEVING YOU ARE WORTHY OF THE TRIP. YOU ARE.

In the grand and profound adventure that is life, the real prize of living courageously is ultimately not what you achieve; it's who you become in the process. Sure, succeeding at your goal — with whatever fame or fortune, accolades or admiration it may bring — can be satisfying and gratifying to the ego. Yet those moments in the spotlight soon fade. What doesn't is knowing that you've given your best, however life has unfolded, and that in the process you've grown into the person you were born to be: imperfect yes, quirky sometimes, but the fullest expression of who you truly are.

ACTION IS THE MOST POWERFUL ANTIDOTE TO FEAR.

You weren't born to have your fears and self-doubt dictate your actions. You were born to soar above them and to become the fullest expression of the potential within you. Don't let it lie dormant by being a passenger in your own life, sitting on the sides, watching it all play out and waiting for some day when the kids are grown, the bills are paid and you've got the clarity and confidence you want to do something. Your life is now. This is it. This is the grand moment, right now. Not tomorrow. Not next week. Not next year.

So step onto centre stage. Own your power. Speak your truth. Blaze your own bright trail and dull your shine for no-one! This world we live in is hungry for people who refuse to surrender to conformity or to sell out to the ranks of mediocrity. It's desperate for people to risk standing out, looking foolish and falling down. It needs what you and only you can bring and it needs the full measure of it. Not a half hedge-your-bets measure. Because when you dare to bring all of who you fully are into your life and start acting more bravely—however seemingly small or insignificant you hold your actions to be—you make the difference only you can make and you inspire others to do the same.

Surely that's worth embracing a little discomfort for?

Take the 'Train the Brave' challenge

Change is never easy, even change for the better. To give you a kickstart on your journey to building your 'courage muscles' in your work, relationships and life, I've created a 10-day video coaching program.

The Train the Brave Challenge is complimentary to everyone who has read *Train the Brave* and would love a little extra support and inspiration. By registering at the link below you'll receive:

» downloadable workbook with a daily progress chart

» daily email in your inbox every day for 10 days, giving you a Train the Brave challenge for that day to keep you in action

» videos of me discussing some of the stories and concepts in this book (plus a few more!)

» automatic subscription to my *Live Bravely!* newsletter

» bonus photos and videos of interviews with people whose stories I've shared!

Sign up now for free at www.TrainTheBrave.com.

Stay brave, stay connected!

We are braver together than we ever could be alone, so let's stay in touch! Please join me wherever you hangout online, where I'll be sharing videos, insights and updates on my public seminars and Live Brave retreat programs.

Facebook.com/margiewarrell

Twitter.com/margiewarrell

Instagram.com/margiewarrell

LinkedIn/in/margiewarrell

YouTube.com/margiewarrell

The Live Brave podcast

Margie's weekly podcast features her insights plus the 'hard won' wisdom of inspiring people from Marianne Williamson to Steve Forbes. Subscribe to listen to Margie each week at **www.TheLiveBravePodcast.com**

The Courage Academy

The Courage Academy offers a host of online courses and other free resources to help you be braver in your work, leadership, relationships and life. To check out the Set Your Life Compass course and the Courageous Conversations Masterclass visit The Courage Academy at **www.CourageAcademy.org**